THE PRE HISTORIC CULTURES
OF
THE MANJRA VALLEY

MEDAK DISTRICT ANDHRA PRADESH

THE PRE HISTORIC CULTURES OF THE MANJRA VALLEY

MEDAK DISTRICT ANDHRA PRADESH

D.L.N. SASTRY
M.A., M.Phil

1997

BHARATIYA KALA PRAKASHAN
DELHI INDIA

Published By:
C.P. Gautam
Bharatiya Kala Prakashan
3611/5, Narang Colony,
Tri Nagar, Delhi-110035
Ph-7192770

First Edition-1997
ISBN : 81–86050–02–7

Laser Typesetting by :–
ISHAN COMPRINT
G-16/14, Qutab Enclave, (DLF)
Phase-I, Gurgaon (Haryana-2)
Ph.: 8-352412

Printed at :–
SANTOSH OFFSET
40, Anand Nagar
Inder Lok, Delhi-110 035

DEDICATED TO

PROF. R. NARASIMHA RAO,
MY TEACHER WHO ILLUMINATED
ME WHILE ENCOURAGING
MY INDIVIDUALITY

CONTENTS

FOREWORD

The valleys of the mighty river Godavari and its tributaries contain considerable importance in Indian Pre-history for the abundant wealth of faunal and lithic artifactual material of the Pre-historic times discovered therein. Since 1950 systematic work on the Stone age in the Godavari basin was carried out by several scholars like Dr. Sankalia, R.V. Joshi and S.N. Raj garu, Carvinus G., Thakur Raja Ram Singh and others. The river Manjra the southern tributary of river Godavari, flows across Maharashtra, North Karnataka and the Western part of Andhra Pradesh covering the border lands. The central portion of Manjra valley covering Medak district was threatened with submersion due to the construction of a dam across the river Manjra at Singoor. The State Department of Archaeology and Museums, was entrusted with the task of surveying and recording of the archaeological wealth of the region. Survey of this basin stretching over 60 Km. between Janwada and Singoor which happens to be the follow up of the previous investigations by Prof. R.V. Joshi and his team, was conducted by Sri D.L.N.Sastry, Assistant Director of this Department during 1982-83.

Besides the investigations into the Pre-historic cultures of the above region, the author discovered and documented several proto historic, early historic and historical sites in this area. It is interesting that the middle reaches of the Manjra Valley explored by the present writer did not yield any evidence pertaining either to the Lower palaeolithic or middle palaeolithic cultures. The Upper palaeolithic industry found in the 40 localities is based on the manufacture of flake tools and blade tools. The thick and broad blade tools suggest primitive stage of tool technology. The predominant element is scraper in the assemblege. So the term "Flake Blade Industry" is appropriate. The author's suggestion of the date range, 20000-10000 years to the Manjra Upper palaeolithic, considering the typological affiliation with the Middle palaeolithic assemblage at Patne, appears to be reasonable.

Following the pattern of other sites in A.P. excepting Kondapur the Manjra Valley is a ceramic and non-geometric in character, consisting of scrapers, borers, burians and points. Similar scenario was reported previously from Karimnagar, Kurnool, Anantapur and Nalgonda. The above factual evidences clearly indicate that the Microlithic industry of Manjra valley is crude and of unsophisticated variety. The observations of the author while comparing the evidence from the industrial complex at Sanganakallu from the chronological aspect seem to be sound and convincing. Therefore the Mesolithic culture of the Manjra valley may be dated to the time bracket between 10000 to 4000 B.C.

But for the life less stone tools, it is unfortunate that none of the sites in the Manjra valley yielded other concomitant finds, to probe in to the cultural horizon of this important and transitary phase in the history of man kind. However we are really fortunate that Sri D.L.N. Sastry has endeavoured for years to discover over 80 sites in a small area under a single river valley system. I heartily congratulate him for the double task of discovery and publication of the results. I am happy to see the first fruit of his incessant labours spread over two decades since the time he joined the department which resulted in the discovery of scores of new sites either pre-historic, proto-historic, early historic or Buddhist which contributed to the enlargement of the canvas of Andhra Culture. I findly hope that this work would impell him to put his other important discoveries in print and prompt other scholars to probe in to the pre-historic cultures of other tributaries of the river Godavary, which will in turn present a comprehensive picture of the Pre-historic Man in A.P. in general and Godavary valley in particular.

Date:
1st July, 1996

Dr. V.V. Krishna Sastry
Former Director
Department of Archaeology & Museums
Govt. of A.P.
Hyderabad

PREFACE

The border lands of Andhra and Maharashtra have been scantily surveyed for purposes of Prehistoric Cultures. The river Manjra which flows across Maharashtra, North Karnataka and the Western part of Andhra Pradesh is ideally suited to trace the cultural contacts of the regions one with the other. Geologically too, the gneissic plateaus of Western Andhra are over looked by the flat topped trapan hills from Maharashtra.

The present work in Medak District covering the central part of the Manjra Valley is a follow up to the investigations carried out in the upper reaches of the same river by Professor R.V. Joshi and his team. An interesting sidelight from this region is the absence of Lower and middle Palaeolithic evidences. The cultural succession begins with Upper Palaeolithic. Mesolithic evidences too are discovered at a number of localities. Close affiliation of these cultures is available at sites both in Maharashtra and Andhra Pradesh.

The present work embodies the results of two seasons, (1983 and 1984) field surveys between Janwada and Singoor, a distance of 60 kms., along the stream, covering the central part of the Manjra Valley. These areas are threatened with submersion by the construction of a dam across the river Manjra at Singoor. The department of Archaeology and Museums, Government of Andhra Pradesh was entrusted with surveying and recording of the archaeological wealth of the regions.

I am deeply indebted to Dr. V.V. Krishna Sastry, former Director of Archaeology and Museums, Government of Andhra Pradesh, for giving me this project work, and writing an encouraging foreword. I am also indebted to Sri N.R.V. Prasad, Director of Archaeology and Museums for his wise counsel and encouragement.

I am very much indebted to Prof. B.R. Subrahmanyam for

his valuable and constant guidance in conducting the field work, collecting data and drafting the present work.

I am thankful to Messrs. P. Dhanunjaya, N. Satyanarayana, P. Satyanarayana, K. Raghunath, P.V. Sharma, K.N. Sagar and Syed Khairul Hussain for their assistance in the field survey. I also thank Mr. E. Appaiah, who shared the trouble in this painstaking village-to village survey.

I express my gratitude to Sri T.Venkatrao, Artist, for the neat drawings and Sri G. Ramesh, Photographer, Visalandhra for his services and to Mr. P. Subba Rao for the decent typing work.

I am also thankful to Sri S. Dasarathi, C.M.O., who always inspired me to undertake works of this kind.

Finally, it is my duty to express my gratitude to my wife, Smt. D.V. Ramana who stood by my side in every respect with deep understanding. In the end, my sincere thanks are to Dr. N.S. Ramachandra Murthy and Smt. B. Indumathi Devi for their help in correcting the proofs with precision and care.

D.L.N. SASTRY

LIST OF FIGURES

LIST OF PLATES

Chapter - I

INTRODUCTORY

The river Manjra is a southern tributary of the river Godavari, joining the latter in the middle reaches of its course. Other important streams joining the middle reaches of Godavari, from the north are Pranahita and Indravati. Other tributaries viz., Purna, Mula, and Pravara join further upstream. The valleys of river Godavari and its tributaries hold considerable importance in Indian Pre-History for the abundant wealth of faunal and lithic artifactual material of the Pleistocene times, discovered therein. The archaeological investigations in the Godavari basin form the back-ground for the present work, ***'The Pre-historic cultures of the Manjra Valley.***

Systematic work on the Stone age in the Godavari basin began in 1950 when Dr. Sankalia studied the sections at Gangapur in Nasik district (Sankalia, H.D. 1952, 74; Sankalia, Deo S.B., & Ansari Z.D. 1960). Godavari and Pravara were repeatedly studied there after, by a number of scholars including R.V. Joshi and S.N. Rajaguru (IAR 1955-56 PP 4-5; IAR 1956-57 PP 11-12; IAR 1957-58 PP 11 & 18; IAR 1959-60 P 12 PP 28-30; IAR 1960-61 PP 22- 23; IAR 1961-62 PP 28-29; IAR 1962-63 P 15; IAR 1963-64 P 22; IAR 1964-65 P 26; IAR 1965-66 P 27; IAR 1967-68 P 31, 32 & 34; IAR 1968-69 PP 13-14; IAR 1969-70 PP 17-18, P 24; IAR 1971-72 PP 31- 32; IAR 1974-75 P 1 ; IAR 1975-76 PP 34-35; IAR 1976-77 PP 38-39; IAR 1977-78 PP 39-40, IAR 1978-79 P 17). Good cliff-sections were observed at Gangapur, Nandoor-Madhmesevar, Kalegaon and Bel- Pandhari (IAR 1959-60). The sections exposed from bottom upwards, a bed of coarse shingle, calcreted gravel with current bedding, brown silt and black-soil. Lower Palaeolithic artifacts were collected in the shingle, whereas middle Palaeolithic ones were available in the cemented gravel. The top of the silt shows a loose kankary-gravel containing microlithic flakes.

Rajaguru noticed in the source region of the river Godavari, nick- points, water-falls, gorges, scarp-faces, pot-holes and such other phenomena, which indicated pleistocene tectonic activity (IAR 1977-78 PP. 39-40). Then followed a phase of strong alluviation. The alluvial fill contained Late Acheulian and Middle Palaeolithic artifacts. At Gangapoor, a representative collection of the Late Acheulian industry was observed. The industry was dominated by oval handaxes and cleavers made of flakes, removed from basaltic dykes, across the river bed. Chirki at Nevasa on the river Pravara provided important evidence of a Late Acheulian primary site (Corvinus, G. 1968). The artifacts were discovered in a 0.7 to 1 m. thick colluvial rubble bed, resting on the uneven surface of rock-bench, carved by water erosion. A cemented sandy gravel horizon (1.6 m. thick) lying on the colluvial rubble bed, yielded Middle Palaeolithic artifacts. The Chirki site yielded a very large number of Acheulian artifacts, over 1700, in an area measuring 270 sq. ms. (IAR 1968-69 PP. 13-14). The tool types comprise hand-axes, cleavers, choppers and scrapers, made on basalt and dolerite. Fossilised tusk of an elephant was a note-worthy find among them.

Joshi (IAR 1969-70 P. 24; IAR 1975-76 PP. 34-35) and Khatri (IAR 1961-62 P. 28) listed several fossiliferous Middle and Late Stone age sites. The Middle Stone Age assemblage consisted of flakes, blades, scrapers, burins, points and prepared flakes, made on chert, agate and jasper. Particularly interesting was the fossil skull of 'Bos', discovered at Kalegaon.

Geomorphic studies carried out in the region of Paithan on the river Godavari indicated that in the past 60,000 to 70,000 years there occurred a vertical shift of the bed level from +20 to -15 m., owing to climatic changes. Middle Palaeolithic artifacts were collected from the 20 m. high ancient channel. The artifacts were dated to a period before 40,000 B.P. on the basis of a corelatable dated evidence from the Mula Dam site at Rahuri. Middle and Upper Palaeolithic artifacts were collected over an extensive area at Bhokar, Sankhutirth and several other places (IAR 1975-76 PP. 34-35).

The river basins drained by Wardha, Wainganga and Pranahita have been extensively surveyed for stone age evidences. At Papaniya- Tekde on Jhorpat, a tributary of Wardha, a succession of Palaeolithic industries, in stratified contexts was observed. (IAR 1961-62 PP. 28-29). Acheulean artifacts comprising of handaxes and cleavers, were picked from the cemented rubble bed, exposed on the river bank. From the upper gravel resting on silt, Middle- Palaeolithic artifacts, including scrapers, borers and miniature hand-axes were collected, whereas the top of the same gravel yielded a blade-burin industry. More or less, the same artifactual evidence in stratified contexts was available at Jhari-Mangrol in the Wainganga basin. Several scores of Palaeolithic and Mesolithic sites have been reported from Wardha-Wainganga basins. Joshi discovered in the upper course of the Wainganga river, two gravel beds, separated by silt. Both the gravel horizons are implementiferous, the lower gravel producing advanced Acheulean types, designated as Wainganga A industry, and the upper gravel giving Middle stone Age artifacts called Wainganga B industry (Joshi 1961, 1964). Allchins consider the Wainganga B industry as distinctively Upper Palaeolithic (Allchins, B. & F.R. 1968).

Thakur Raja Ram Singh painstakingly explored the Adilabad- Karimnagar - Warangal - Khammam stretch of the Godavari basin and discovered several fossiliferous stone age sites, which yield a fund of information on the late Pleistocene ecology and human occupation of the region. The litho-units of the exposed cliff sections are marked by gravels, with intercalations of highly calcreted silts/clays. Acheulean sites have been encountered in a 300 Sq. Km. area, which concentrated, occurrences focusing on Ramagundam and Godavari Khani situations (IAR 1974-75 P. 1; K.N. Prasad and Raja Ram Singh APJA P. 7-29; APJA PP. 59-62).

Middle and Upper Palaeolithic sites are more widely distributed in the region. Particularly interesting are two Upper Palaeolithic sites at Wankhed and Manikgudem in Adilabad district. At Wankhed, there were 333 finished lithic artifacts and 42 dental and bone remains. Manikgudem, on the other hand yielded 61 stone tools and 219 faunal remains. The author interprets that the former was a settlement site and the latter a butchering place. The Late Pleistocene horizons contained a wide variety of faunal remains including Bos, Bubalus, Equus, Equus asius, Gazellinae, Caprinae and Sudi besides rodents. The ecological setting indicated was, open woodland - of savannah type.

MANJRA BASIN

The occurrence of stone age artifacts in the Manjra basin was first reported by A.V. N. Murthy in the year 1957-58. He reported the discovery of series II tools and microliths at Appareddipalli and Satwar in Zahirabad taluq, district Medak (IAR 1957-58 P. 11). More important evidence was available in 1971-'72 when Bopardikar systematically explored the upper reaches of the Manjra. At six places - Ambajogai, Kalliam, Deoli, Tadul, Wagdari and Sirsa, he discovered fossiliferous deposits in the ancient channels of the Manjra river. At three places-Kalliam, Deoli and Tadul, he was able to find Middle and Late Stone Age artifacts on surface and in re-deposited contexts. The artifacts, mostly flakes, scrapers, blades etc., were fashioned on chert, chalcedony and agate. The stratigraphy at nearly all the places, consists of 0.70 to 0.80m., thick sandy gravel resting on bed-rock and overlain by redeposited black soil mixed with lime concretions. The gravel bed was fossiliferous containing Elephas and Bos. The black soil horizon contained plenty of Molluscan shells. The same area was reexplored by R.V. Joshi and his associates in 1975-'76. They also reported evidence for shifting of river course. The stratigraphy consisted of calcreted pebble gravel overlain by brownish silty sandy clay. The pebble gravel probably represented an ancient braided course of the Manjra. The gravel horizon was richly fossiliferous. The animals represented were buffaloes *(Bubalus bubalis),* deer *(Cervussp),* horse *(Equus namadicus)* and cattle *(Bos namadicus)* already reported. The top silty clay was essentially a low energy deposit characteristic of stream meanders and ox-bow lake formations in the old flood plain. In a fresh survey carried out in 1981 more of fossil evidence has been reported. For the first time remains of Hippopotamus sp. was discovered. R.M. Shadakshariah reported 21 Middle Stone Age and 11 Microlithic sites in Bidar district.

The reported surveys carried out in the upper reaches of the Manjra Valley pointed to rich fossil evidence, but on the whole, the pre-historic artifactual evidences are quite unimpressive. The fossils indicate open woodland - savannah environment with occasional marshes, developing in low level zones.

REFERENCES

Allchin, Bridget & Raymond 1968 *The Birth of Indian Civilization* pp.61-62.

Corvinus, G. 1968 'An Acheulean Occupation floor at Chirki-on-Pravara, India,' *Current Athropology,* pp.216-18.

Joshi, R.V. 1961 Stone Age Industries in the Upper Wainganga Basin, Maharashtra State. *Proceedings 48th Ind. Sc. Congress,* Part III p.447.

1964 Acheulean Succession in Central India, *Asian Prespectives,* pp.150-63.

1981 Archaeological sites in the Manjra Valley. Central Godavari basin, *Bulletin of the Deccan College Research Institute,* Poona.

Prasad, K.N. & T.R. Singh 1984 Observations on the Vertibrate Fossils from Karimnagar and Adilabad Districts, A.P., *The Andhra Pradesh Journal of Archaeology, Vol.II No.1* pp.59-62.

Sankalia, H.D.	1952	*The Godavari Palaeolithic Industry,* Poona.
- Deo, S.B. & Ansari, Z.D	1960	*From History to Prehistory at Nevasa,* Poona
Sankalia, H.D.	1974	*Prehistory and Protohistory of India and Pakistan,* Poona (First Edition 1962-63, New Edition 1974).
Singh, T.R.	1984	Living conditions of Palaeolithic Man in Godavari Valley rom Basar to Bhadrachalam, A.P., India, *The Andhra Pradesh Journal of Archaeology, Vol. II No. 1.* pp. 7-29.

Chapter - II

PHYSICAL BACKGROUND

The river Manjra drains the Medak and Nizamabad districts in Andhra Pradesh. These two districts lie adjacent to the borders of Maharashtra and Karnataka. The region has a general altitude of 500 mm., above the M.S.L. and forms part of the Deccan Plateau. For the purpose of present study, the river Manjra from Janwada to Singoor, a distance of about 60 kms has been surveyed.

The Medak district furnishes the picture of an undulating land surface, occasionally featured by groups of hillocks. There are no prominent hill ranges traversing the district. Two ranges of hills however need mention. One of them i.e. the Ramayampet range covers the northern and southern parts of Nizamabad district. The other range enters from the north-western corner and continues east-wards upto Medak town.

The district is drained by Manjra and its tributary streams. Among them only two streams are worthy of mention. One of them, viz. Dabbavagu joins Manjra at Singoor and the other Haldi near Medak. The river Manjra which is an important tributary of Godavari, takes birth in Balaghat plateau at Patoda, at an altitude of 823 m. and flows through Osmanabad and Bidar districts, before entering Medak at Janwada. In Medak district, it flows for a length of 96 kms., through Narayan Khed, Zahirabad, Sangareddi, Narsapoor and Medak taluqs before continuing its course in the Nizamabad district, to join the river Godavari near Bodhan.

The undulated topography of the region favoured formation of numerous nullahs and as many as 61 tanks.

The area is predominant in granitic gneiss of the Archaean

age. There are inlier bands, patches and lenses of schists, quartzites and carbonate rocks. One can see the exposure of these near Siddipet. Further the granitic gneiss is traversed across by pigmatites, quartz-veins and dolerite dykes. The south-western part of the district including Sangareddi taluq is covered by Deccan trap. The granitic gneiss which is the country rock of the area occurs in various forms such as hills, tors, domes and boulders. The Deccan trap formations on the other hand take the form of flat topped hills. Crypto-Crystalline silica such as chalcedony, agate, chert and jasper occur as amygdales in the trap formations.

The soils are mostly red-earths comprising loamy sands and sandy clays, except on river banks and in the valleys. In Zahirabad taluq, lateritic soils predominate. Along the river channels, black-cotton soils, particularly clay loams and silty clays are spread extensively. The black soils are alkaline, with high soluble salt content. Soil erosion due to undulating topography and surface run off has led to severe gullying, especially in the marginal lands bordering on hillocks.

The climate of the area may be termed as dry-tropical monsoonal. In mid-summer, especially in the month of May, the mean maximum temperature often crosses 42°C and the minimum averages at 26°C.December which is the coldest month of the year records a mean maximum temperature of 29°C and the mean minimum of 14°C. But occasionally temperatures as low as 6°C are also recorded. The average rainfall for the district is 896.7 mm., and the number of rainy days is 54. But the rainfall records for the last 50 years show considerable variation between 600 and 1,100 mm.

Medak district, like most other parts of Andhra Pradesh, is much depleted of its natural vegetation, by overgrazing and deforestation. The forest type is classified under the head southern-tropical-dry-deciduous, dominated by Acacia-sendra *(Sundra) Soymidia, Febribuga (Somi), Boswella, Serrata (Erramaddi)*. Some ever green species - Ixora Parviflora *(Korivi),* Memeoylon edula *(Alli*) and Minusops hexandra *(Sapota)* are found intermixed with the dry deciduous ones. The forests generally have two storeys, the upper canopy rising to a maximum of 12 to 15 m. height being uneven and not very close.

The common species in the top storey consist of Tectona garandis, Anogeissus latifolia *(Chirumanu)*, Lager-stroemia Parviflora *(Chennangi)*, Terminalia tomentosa *(Maddi)*, Terminalia *(Arjuna)*, Pterocarpus marsupium *(Yegi)*, Chloroxylon suietenia *(Satin or Tellabitlu)*, Diospyros melonoxylon *(Tunki)*, Latifolia *(Mohwa or Eppa)*, Boswellia serrata *(Anduga)*, Sterculia urens *(Tapsi or Kavali)*, Lannea garandis *(Gumpena)*, Salmalia Malbaricum *(Burugu)*, Dalbergia latifolia *(Shisham or Jittegi)*, Dalbergia paniculata *(Sopera)* and Soymida Febrifuga. The lower canopy consists of cleistanthus collinus *(Kodsha or Kodesa)*, Emblica Officinalis *(Amla or Usiri)*, Acacia-sundra, Mimusops hexandra Memecylon edule, Zizyphus zylopyrus *(Gotti)*, Buchanamia latifolia *(Chironji)*, Cassia fixtula *(Amaltas or rela)*, Ixora Parviflora, Gardenia lucidi *(Karinga or Dikamalli)* and Santalum album *(Sandal)* and occurs only in Zhirabad range. The common shrubs, namely, Cassia auriculate *(Tangedu)*, Holarrhena antidysenterica *(Istaripala)*, Grewia hirsuta (Tellajana), Woodfordea floribunda *(Jaji)* and Nyclanthes arbortristis *(Parijata)* occupy the ground storey. The common climbers found in the forests are Butea superba *(Belpalas or Tigamoduga)*, Acaciaintsia *(Korints)* and Calycopteris floribunda *(Bonthatiga)*. Thick mats of grass are often met with in these forests during the rainy season. The common grasses are Cymbopogan Mastini *(Kachigaddi)*, Artistida adsecensioris *(Pillipesara gaddi)*, Andropogon concortus *(Eddigaddi)* and Cynodon dactylon (Garikigaddi). Some of these plants are edible and must have been used for food by the prehistoric people as well.

There has been a considerable destruction of the wild fauna in the district. The tiger which was once a pride of the forest is almost non-existing. In the deep jungles of Narsapoor, Medak and Ramayampet, traces of leopard and Hyaena are noticeable. The wolf, jackal and the fox are a common site on the forest fringes. Herds of wild-bear are usually found in deep jungles. The black-buck, the four-horned antelope, sambar and cheetal (spotted deer) roam about the more open grass lands. The wild dog, pocharam and mangoose are quite common. Among the avifauna, partridge, pigeon, sand-grouse, the great Indian bustard, pea foul, green pigeon, green jungle fowl and a variety of ducks and cranes are the common birds. The seasonal availability of vegetal food stuffs and the wide variety of fauna, not to speak of the aqua fauna, must have attracted the prehistoric man to the Manjra basin.

It should be clear from the above that, from March to December there is seasonal availability of vegetal food stuffs. There must be many other food plants than the few listed above.

REFERENCES

Medak	1976	Andhra Pradesh District Gazetteers
Dutt, N.V.B.S.	1981	*Geology and Mineral Resources of Andhra Pradesh,* Hyderabad.
Small, R.J.	1978	*The Study of Landforms,* Cambridge. (First Edition 1970, Second Edition 1978)
Spate, O.H.K.	1954	*India and Pakistan:* A General and Regional Geography, London.
Wadia, D.N.	1976	*Geology of India,* New Delhi, Fourth Edition.

Chapter - III

SITES

The Manjra river valley was explored by the present writer between Janwada and Singoor (Fig. 1. Pl. 1) a distance of over 60 Kms. The area explored was due for submersion owing to the construction of a dam across the river, at Singoor. At Janwada the river Manjra enters Andhra Pradesh. In the explored stretch, the river maintains a low graded profile, registering a fall of not more than 20 metres. The present Manjra river is a low energy stream with 2 to 4 cusecs of discharge in the lean season and 250 cusecs when in spate. Some fifty wet weather streams of different sizes join the course of Manjra.

At several points along the course, particularly at Singoor, Raipalli and Murtuzapoor, the river preserves two erosional terraces covered by thin fluvial deposits. At Singoor, the terraces measure 18 mts. and 6 mts. high respectively above the present water level. (Fig. 2. Pl. - 2). At Chalki, a transverse stream cuts cross the higher terrace, exposing a thin sheet of sandy gravel covered by brownish clay silt. Black earth of uneven thickness constitutes the top layer of the cliff section. Calcareous nodules (Kankar) are present on the surface of black earth. The lower terrace is composed of redeposited black-earth, resting on rock. The sandy gravel was the channel deposit of the ancient stream. The river, since depositing black earth, rejuvenated its course and severly cut its bed deeper into the rock. The river now flows on bare rock and there are rock exposures along the banks. Upper Palaeolithic artifacts in fresh condition occur on both the terraces and it would appear that the river Manjra had stabilised in its present course by the time the Upper Palaeolithic men were present in the area.

A total of 40 prehistoric sites were discovered in two seasons' field survey. The sites are either Upper Palaeolithic or Mesolithic or both. The artifactual yield at many of the sites is meagre. At only two localities viz. Raipalli and Murtuzapoor there is a sizeable collection. The site at Murtuzapoor is quite rich with hundreds of Upper Palaeolithic tools collected, besides many more left behind.

Stone age sites are present on both the terraces. But the Upper Palaeolithic and Microlithic artifacts on the higher terrace are a little fresh and unworn than they are on the lower. Faint indications of water action seen on the specimens from T2 may be attributed to local shuffling.

In the following pages, the various sites and the artifactual material collected from each of them are listed. The order in which the sites are presented follows the course of the river Manjra.

1. *CHIKURTI* : (CKT 77° 37'E/17° 54'N)

This site is situated at half-a kilometre distance to the south of the village on the right bank of the river. Artifacts were collected from the surface of the older terrace (T_1). The artifacts are fresh and unworn and comprise of both Upper Palaeolithic and Mesolithic implements.

UPPER PALAEOLITHIC

1. Convex scraper
2. Transverse scraper
3. Side cum hollow scraper
4. Blade blank.

MESOLITHIC

1. Backed piece on flake
2. Retouched flake

2. *KAKI JANWADA* : (KJW 77° 40'E/17° 57'N)

The site is located at a distnce of a kilometre to the north of the village and one and a half kilometres away from the right bank of the river. Both Upper Palaeolithic and Mesolithic artifacts were collected on the site.

The artifacts are fresh and unworn.

UPPER PALAEOLITHIC	MESOLITHIC
1. Convex scrapers	1. Flake
2. Blade	2. Backed piece
3. End scraper	3. Borer
	4. Flake blank

3. *MURTUZAPOOR* : (MZP 77° 40'E/17° 56'N)

This is the most important among the sites discovered in the Manjra valley. Here, there is an abundance of upper Palaeolithic artifactual material. Chert outcrops (P1.3) in the form of boulders and bands all over the area account for the prolific occurrence of artifacts. Chert boulders (P1.3) bear chipped marks and there is little doubt that tool manufacture was locally done. The site has been under cultivation and as such there must have occurred local shuffling of artifacts. Yet it is possible to observe clusters of artifacts in the immediate vicinity of the raw-material exposures. The site is extensive and the tools are widely scattered in fields, adjacent to the north and south of the village.

There are large quantities of both finished and unfinished tools available on the site, as such, it may be categorised as factory cum settlement site. From this it is possible to surmise that the prehistoric men took advantage of natural exposures of chert and chose to settle at the place.

Though repeated tillage of the surface soil has caused considerable disturbance, attempt has been made to identify floor patches. At least two of them are recognisable and one with relatively less disturbed outlines measures 2.6 m. x 1.5 m. (P1.3). As many as 1850 specimens of finished and unfinished tools were counted within a radius of 5 m. around an exposed chert boulder.

A rain gully adjacent to the site shows weathered rock covered by black earth. It is from the surface of the black earth that the collection of artifacts was entirely made (Fig. 3B, Pl. 2). The artifact types are noted below.

Artifact Types	Blade	Flake (0) (P)	Core	Total
1. Retouched	7	7 + 7	—	21
2. Scrapers :				
(a) Side	2	5 + 0	—	7
(b) End	1	3 + 0	—	4
(c) Convex	—	4 + 7	1	12
(d) Hollow	—	2 + 2	—	4
(e) Side cum End	—	1 + 0	—	1
3. Borers	—	1 + 0	1	2
4. Scraper cum borers	—	2 + 0	—	2
5. Backed pieces	13	—	—	13
6. Points	—	1 + 1	—	2
Others :				
Cores	—	—	5	5
Prepared Cores	—	—	2	2
Flakes	—	17	—	17
Flake blanks	—	5	—	5
Blade blanks	9	—	—	9
Rejects	—	—	—	50

4. *ATMYAL* : (ATL 77°40'E/ 17°59'N)

The site is located adjacent to the village and a kilometre away from the left bank of the river. Only two microliths were collected at the place.

1. Fluted Core - 1
2. Side Scraper - 1

5. *BADALGAON* : (BDG 77°42'E / 17°59'N)

The site lies half a kilometre to the west of the village and one and a-half kilometre away from the left bank of the river. A nullah flows close by the site. Artifacts were found scattered over a wide area and a random collection made on the site includes the following *Upper Palaeolithic* tool types.

1. Side scraper
2. Convex scrapers on flake - 2
3. Side cum end scraper on blade
4. Backed pieces - 3

6. *PULAKURTI* : (PKT 77°43'E / 17°57'N)

The site is situated 1.5 kms. away from the left bank of the river by the side of the pathway between the village and the ford point. Artifacts of Upper Palaeolithic and Mesolithic were found scattered over a fairly extensive area and the following tools were collected.

UPPER PALAEOLITHIC

1. Blade blank
2. Scraper cum borer
3. Convex scraper
4. Side cum hollow scraper
5. Flake core.

MESOLITHIC

1. Convex scraper on blade
2. Side scrapers on blade

7. *BELLAPUR* : (BLP 77°47'E / 17°56'N)

The site is situated close to the western side of the village and a kilometre away from the left bank of the river. Here several Upper Palaeolithic artifacts and a few Microliths were noticed. The following are the specimens collected from the site.

UPPER PALAEOLITHS	**MICROLITHS**
1. Side scraper	1. Flake blank
2. Side cum end scraper	
3. Blade	
4. Backed piece	
5. Flake Blank.	

8. *CHALKI* : (CLK 77°40'E / 17°55'N)

The site is situated to the north of the village and a kilometre away from the right bank of the river. A streamlet flows close by the site. Here both Upper Palaeoliths and Microliths occur. They are slightly rolled, probably due to stream action. Collected tools are as follows :

UPPER PALAEOLITHS	**MICROLITHS**
1. Backed piece	1. Scraper cum borer
	2. Flake Blanks

9. *RAGHAVAPUR* : (RGP 77°40'E / 17°50'N)

The site lies a Kilometre to the south-east of the village on the way to Matoor. The river Manjra flows nearly 2 kms. away from the place. A nullah flows close by. Tools were collected from the surface of the black earth. They consist of the following :

UPPER PALAEOLITHS	**MICROLITHS**
1. Backed blade	1. Scraper cum borer
2. Hollow scraper on flake	2. Hollow scraper
3. Blade.	

10. *MATOOR* : (MTR 77°46'E / 17°54'N)

The site is located on the rightbank of the river Manjra and close to the village. Both Upper Palaeoliths and Microliths were found on the surface of the black earth in terrace - 1.

UPPER PALAEOLITHS

1. Point
2. Single shouldered point
3. Hollow scrapers
4. Side scraper on flake
5. Flake blank.

MICROLITHS

1. Point on blade
2. Borers on flake
3. Side Scraper on blade
4. Blade blanks

11. *KHANJABALPUR* : (KJB 77°41'E / 17°50'30N")

Situated to the north of the village, the site lies one Kilometre away from the river on terrace-1. *Upper Palaeolithic* artifacts were collected on the surface of the black earth. The tools are fresh and unworn.

1. Flakes
2. Blade blank
3. Backed blade
4. End scraper
5. Convex scraper on flake
6. Core.

12. PAMPAD : (PPD 77° 46'8"E / 17° 54'34"N)

The site is situated at a distance of a kilometre to the west of the village on terrace -1 and one and a half Kilometres from the river. The artifacts belong to the *Upper Palaeolithic* period and look fresh. Tools collected are :

1. Backed piece

2. Burin
3. Side Scraper
4. Flake

13. *SIRUR* : (SRR 77°47'17"E / 17°53'17"N)

The site is situated on the right bank of Manjra and adjacent to the western side of the village. Upper Palaeolithic and Microlithic artifacts were collected from the black earth of terrace-1. The tools collected were fresh and unworn.

UPPER PALAEOLITHS	**MICROLITHS**
1. Blades	1. Flake blank
2. Point on blade	
3. Side scraper.	

14. *DOWLATABAD* : (DTB 77°47'52"E / 17°52'34"N)

This is both an Upper Palaeolithic and Microlithic site, situated a kilometre away from the right bank of Manjra. The path way leading to Mamidipalli passes by its side. The artifacts collected include:

UPPER PALAEOLITHS	**MICROLITHS**
1. Blade	1. Convex scraper
2. Burin.	2. Blade blank.

15. *PIPPALAPALLI* : (PPL 77°47'E / 17°51'42"N)

This site is predominantly a Microlithic site situated on terrace-1, a kilometre and a half away from the right bank of the river and more or less at the same distance to the north-east of the village. Upper Palaeolithic and Microlithic artifacts collected are —

UPPER PALAEOLITHS

1. Convex scraper on flake
2. Backed piece

MICROLITHS

1 Fluted core
2. Flake blanks
3. Side scrapers on blade

16. *RAIPALLI* : (RPL 77°48'17"E / 17°53'17"N)

This is one of the two sites where a sizeable number of both Upper Palaeolithic and Microlithic artifacts were available (P1.4). The stone tools were found scattered on the surface of the black earth over an extensive area to the north and east of the village. The artifacts look fresh and unworn. At two spots the Microliths were found to occur in clusters, suggesting the occurrence of prehistoric homesteds. But intensive tillage of the surface soil has irretrievably damaged all traces of their outlines. However, Raipalli may be considered as one of the important localities so far as the artifactual yield is concerned. The rain gullies which cut across the area have exposed from bottom upwards weathered rock superimposed by black earth of varying thickness. The black earth contains calcarious nodules and occasionally lateritic pellets. (Fig. 3A). In the river bed, bare rock and redeposited pebbly gravel were exposed. (P1.4).

Details of **Microlithic tools** collected in the vicinity of Raipalli are as follows:

1. Burin on blade - 1
2. Borer on blade - 1
3. Borers on flake - 2
4. Borer cum scraper - 1
5. Convex scrapers on flake - 2
6. Hollow scrapers on flake - 3
7. Hollow scrapers on blade - 2
8. Side scrapers on flake - 4
9. Side cum end scraper on blade - 1
10. Blades - 4
11. Blade blanks - 4
12. Flake blanks - 1
13. Backed piece on core - 1
14. Backed pieces on blade - 2
15. Backed pieces on flake - 2
16. Ordinary cores - 2
17. Fluted cores - 12

Table showing Upper Palaeolithic and Microlithic artifacts collected from the vicinity of Raipalli.

Artifacts	Blade	Flake	Core	Total
1. Scrapers :				
(a) side	3	6(2 Mic)	—	9
(b) End	—	—	—	—
(c) Hollow	1	8(3 Mic)	—	9
(d) Convex	—	7(2 Mic)	—	7
(e) Side cum end	—	—	1	1
2. Borers :				
(a) Scraper cum borer		—	1	1
3. Burin	1(Mic)	—	—	1
4. Blades	4(3 Mic)	—	—	4
5. Backed pieces	2	2	3	7
6. Points	1	1(Mic)	—	1
7. Retouched flakes	—	5	—	5
Others :				
Cores	—	—	3(Up1)	3
Blade cores	—	—	10(Mic)	10
Flake blanks	—	6(4 Mic)	—	6
Blade Blanks	5(2 Mic)	—	—	5
Rejects	—	—	—	140

17. *GATTPAL* : (GPL 77° 48'17"E / 17° 53'30"N)

It lies about 5 Kilometres to the north of Raipalli and is situated on the right bank as Raipalli. Here, the site yielded both Upper Palaeolithic and Mesolithic tools. They occur in the same context as at Raipalli. The following are the types.

UPPER PALAEOLITHS	MICROLITHS
1. Flake blanks	1. Side scraper on blade
2. Backed pieces	2. Flake blanks

18. *JUNGLE HUSIRIKAPALLI* : (JKP 77°49'18"E / 17°53'10"N)

The tool bearing locality of the site is located about half a kilometre away from the left bank of the river and one kilometre to the south of the village. A majority of Upper Palaeolithic artifacts and few microliths occur on the site. They occur in the same context as at the preceding site.

UPPER PALAEOLITHS	MICROLITHS
1. Convex scraper	1. Blade blanks
2. Blade	
3. Side Scrapers	
4. Transverse Scraper	

19. *PALADUGU* : (PLG 77°50'48"E / 17°52'8"N)

The site is located close to a stony waste land covered with bouldary spreads. A deep stream flows nearby, cutting across the terrain. The section exposed, from bottom upwards, weathered rock and black-earth. This is predominantly an Upper Palaeolithic site. A meagre number of Microliths were also available.

UPPER PALAEOLITHS	MICROLITHS
1. Amorphous core	1. Backed piece on blade
2. Borer on flake	
3. Flake blanks	
4. Hollow scraper on flake	
5. Backed piece	
6. Blade blank.	

20. *DEVANOOR* : (DVR 77°51'17"E / 17°52'50"N)

Situated on a small rocky outcrop, the site lies about 2 kms., away from the left bank of the river and one km., to the west of the village. A streamlet flows close by. A number of **microliths** were found on the surface. The artificts collected include :

1. Backed piece
2. Flake
3. Convex Scraper
4. Backed Blade

21. *BUTKUR* : (BTR 77°52'25"E / 17° 52'50"N)

The place is situated about 2 kms., from the river Manjra. Artifacts were collected on the surface of black-earth. A small nullah flows close by. Some of the artifacts were found in a slightly rolled condition. It may be due to local shuffling. The tools are all **Upper Palaeolithic :**

1. Convex Scraper on Flake
2. Convex cum hollow scraper on flake
3. End scraper on thick flake
4. End scraper on blade
5. Hollow scraper
6. Round scraper on core.

22. *GORREKAL* : (GRK 77°53'50"E / 17°53'25"N)

It is an extensive site situated about 2 kms., away from the bank of the river and more or less the same distance to the south-east of the village. Shallow wet weather streamlets flow nearby the site. It is mainly an Upper Palaeolithic site and the tools are fresh and unrolled. Few microliths were also available. The collected tools are as below:

UPPER PALAEOLITHS	**MICROLITHS**
1. Flake	1. Flakes
2. Incomplete blade	
3. Hollow scraper	
4. Convex scraper	
5. Blades	
6. Flake	
7. Core	

23. *DARKASPALLI* : (DKP 77°53'4"E / 17°52'8"N)

The tool bearing locality is situated about half a kilometre west of the village and a kilometre and half from the left bank of the river. Shallow wet weather streams flow nearby. Tools both Upper Paleolithic and Microlithic were found and the collection made includes :

UPPER PALAEOLITHS	**MICROLITHS**
1. Backed piece	1. Backed pieces on blade
2. Convex Scraper	2. Flake blank
3. Borer on flake	3. Borer on flake

24. *GOWTAPOOR* : (GTP 77° 54' 8"E / 17° 51' 8"N)

The site is situated 2 kms., to the south-west of the village and more or less at the same distance from the left bank of the river Manjra. Two shallow streamlets flow in the vicinity. Upper Palaeolithic and Micro-lithic artifacts are scattered over an extensive area. The tools collected are :

UPPER PALAEOLITHS	**MICROLITHS**
1. Blade	1. Fluted core
2. Backed piece on flake	2. Borer on flake

3. Hollow scraper on blade	3. Points on blade
4. Flake	4. Blade
5. Blade Blank	

25. *HUSIRIKAPALLI* : (HKP 77° 52'25"E / 17°51'34"N)

The site lies about half a kilometre to the north of the village on terrace-2, and a kilometre from the left bank of the river. Upper Palaeolithic and Microlithic artifacts were found scattered over wide area. Collection made on the site includes :

UPPER PALAEOLITHS	MICROLITHS
1. Blade blanks	1. Fluted core
2. Backed pieces	
3. Double shouldered point on flake.	

26. *INDOOR* : (IND 77°50'42"E / 17°51'17"N)

The site is situated a Kilometre to the east of the village on terrace -2 of the river Manjra. Shallow rain channels flow close by in the vicinity. Upper Palaeolithic and Microlithic artfacts were found on the surface over an extensive area. Tools collected from the site are as follows :

UPPER PALAEOLITHS	MICROLITHS
1. Borers	1. Fluted core
2. Flakes	

27. *NIRJAPPALA* : (NJP 77°52'17"E / 17°50'52"N)

The tool bearing locality is situated just to the north of the village on terrace-2 of the left bank of the river Manjra. Both Upper Palaeolithic and Microlithic artifacts were found scattered over a small area. The artifacts appear to be slightly water worn. The collection is as follows :

UPPER PALAEOLITHS

1. Backed pieces
2. Side scraper
3. Flake
4. Simple flakes

MICROLITHS

1. Fluted core
2. Borer on blade

28. *BOGULAMPALLI* : (BMP 77°50'42"E / 17°49'42"N)

The site is situated on terrace-2, half a Kilometre away from the right bank of the river. The village lies a kilometre to the west of the site. It is a **Mesolithic site** and the few artifacts collected are as here under

1. Fluted core.

29. *KHADIRABAD* : (KDB 77°54'43"E / 17°49'42"N)

The site at this place is situated closeby a stony waste land characterised by boulder exposures. Two rain water streamlets flow nearby, cutting across the terrain. The section exposed from botom upwards comprises weathered rock and black earth. The site is located 2 kms., south-west of the village on terrace-2 and by the side of the pathway leading to the ferry. Upper Palaeolithic and Microlithic artifacts were found in a slightly rolled condition on the surface of black earth. A few tools collected from the site are :

UPPER PALAEOLITHS

1. Side scraper on flake
2. Backed piece
3. Flake blank

MICROLITHS

1. Fluted core

30. *KODUR* : (KDR 77°52'E / 17°49'8"N)

The tool bearing locality is situated about a kilometre to the south-east of the village, by the side of the path-way, leading to the ferry. A small rain gully flows on the southern fringe of the site. The section exposed contains black earth. The artifacts were found over a wide area, on the surface of terrace-2. The artifacts collected are as follows :

UPPER PALAEOLITHS

1. Double edged side scraper on blade
2. Side scraper on blade
3. Blade
4. Borer on flake

MICROLITHS

1. Side scraper on blade
2. Backed piece on flake

31. *BELUR* : (BLR 77°53'42"E / 17°48'N)

The site lies on terrace-2 on the right bank of Manjra and a kilometre to the south of the village. Adjacent to the site is a stony waste land. Both Upper Palaeolithic and Microlithic artifacts occur in a semi rolled condition over a wide area. Artifacts collected from the site are as follows :

UPPER PALAEOLITHS

1. Backed pieces
2. Hollow scraper
3. Flake
4. 'D' Shaped scraper

MICROLITHS

1. Core
2. Hollow scraper
3. Flake blanks

32. *MANTOOR* : (MTR 77° 55'25"E / 17°47'34"N)

The tool bearing locality lies in terrace-2. Artifacts were found over a wide area, located half a kilometre north-west of the village. The few artifacts collected from the site are as follows:

UPPER PALAEOLITHS
1. Side scraper
2. Hollow scraper
3. Blade blank
4. Burin

MICROLITHS
1. Blade blank
2. Hollow scraper on flake
3. Side scraper on blade

33. *KALLEPALLI* : (KPL 77°53'25"E / 17°47'17"N)

Situated on an elevated portion, the site lies on the right bank of the river and a kilometre to the south-east of the village. Upper Palaeolithic and Microlithic artifacts were found scattered on the surface of black-earth. *Upper Palaeoliths* predominate. The collection of artifacts from the surface is as follows :

1. Hollow scraper on flake
2. Blade Blank
3. Flake
4. Amorphous core
5. Backed piece
6. End scraper.

34. *HONNAPUR* : (HNP 77°55'25"E / 17°46' 25"N)

It is predominantly a Mesolithic site situated a kilometre to the north-west of the village. Upper Palaeolithic and Microlithic artifacts in a slightly rolled condition were found on the surface of terrace-2. The collected specimens are :

UPPER PALAEOLITHS
1. End Scraper
2. Borer

MICROLITHS
1. Fluted cores
2. Blade blanks

35. *REGULAPAD* : (RPD 77°54'17"E / 17°46'17"N)

This place is situated one Kilometre away from the right bank of the river. The surface of terrace-2 is strewn with Upper Palaeolithic and Mesolithic artifacts. The few tools collected are as noted below:

UPPER PALAEOLITHS

1. Convex scraper on core
2. Point

MICROLITHS

1. Borer on flake
2. Borer cum scraper
3. Hollow cum scraper
4. Blade
5. Backed piece on flake
6. Ordinary core.

36. *SER PEDAREDDIPET* : (SRP 77°56'34"E / 17°46'17"N)

The site is situated a kilometre to the west of the village by the side of the path-way leading to Honnapaur. It is predominantly an Upper Palaeolithic site. But few microliths are also available. The tools were slightly water worn. Artifacts collected are :

UPPER PALAEOLITHS

1. Borer
2. Double edged blade
3. Side scraper
4. Blade blank

MICROLITHS

1. Borer on blade

37. *KESARAM*: (KSM 77°53'17"E / 17°45'34"N)

This is predominantly a Mesolithic site situated on terrace-2 of the river. A rock outcrop, close by, is littered with microlithic artifacts. Tools collected are as shown below :

UPPER PALAEOLITHS	MICROLITHS
1. Blade	1. Fluted core
	2. Blade blank
	3. Flake blank
	4. Hollow Scraper on flake

38. *RAMACHANDRAPURAM* : (RCM 77°50'34"E / 17°45'17"N)

The site located is on terrace-2 and 2 kms. to the north-east of the village. Both Upper Palaeolithic and microlithic artifacts were present. But the latter predominate. Tools collected are as shown under :

UPPER PALAEOLITHS	MICROLITHS
1. Side scraper cum borer on blade	1. Borer on flake
2. Backed blade	2. Blade blanks
3. Flake	3. Flake blank
4. Convex scraper	4. Borer cum scraper
	5. Side scraper on blade
	6. Backed piece on core
	7. Backed pieces on flake

39. *BASIREDDIPALLI* : (BRP 77°55'34"E / 16°59'43"N)

The site is situated adjacent to a low hill ridge, on the right bank of Manjra, where it is joined by a perennial stream, Dabbavagu. The site lies 2 kms. south of the village. In the slopes of the ridge, Upper Palaeolithic and Microlithic artifacts were found. The tools collected are as follows :

UPPER PALAEOLITHS	MICROLITHS
1. Core	1. Blade blank

2. Blade blank
3. Backed blade
4. Side scraper
5. Point

2. Borer on flake
3. Side scraper on flake

40. *SINGOOR* : (SGR 77°56'30"E / 17°45'7"N)

The site is situated on terrace-2 of the river and a kilometre to the south of the village. Both Upper Palaeolithic and Microlithic artifacts were collected. The former are more in number. The tools collected are as listed below :

UPPER PALAEOLITHS

1. Flakes
2. Point on flake
3. Hollow scraper
4. Side cum end scraper

MICROLITHS

1. Flake

In the 60 kms. stretch of the river course explored between Janwada and Singoor, 40 sites have been discovered. Among these, 7 sites have provided exclusively Upper Palaeolithic evidences, 3 exclusively Mesolithic, where as the remaining 30 yeilded both Upper Palaeolithic and Mesolithic artifactual material. These sites are more or less uniformly distributed in the valley. The preponderant number of sites yielding both Upper Palaeolithic and Mesolithic artifacts indicates that the same spots served the interests of both the cultures equally. This would lead to the inference that either the foraging practices or the bio-physical environment or both did not undergo much change from the Upper Palaeolithic to the Mesolithic times. The river, more or less, stabilised in its present course by the time the Upper Palaeolithic men were present in the area. Stable river course over a long period of time would indicate little change in climate and bio-physical environment. Any changes that may have occurred in the climate and the river course subsequently were only marginal. This probably accounts for the presence of both Upper Palaeolithic and Mesolithic sites on both the terraces. More of water wear noticed on some of the artifacts occurring in terrace-2 may be attributed to local shuffling caused either by occasional excessive floods or lateral flows of rain water from higher grounds. Recurrence of severe floods is not an unknown phenomenon in the river Manjra. In the year 1983 there occurred a severe flood, with 6.500 cusecs of discharge. Such severe floods were even recorded in 1953 and 1959.

The survey indicated that the artifacts, though widely scattered over the area, occur only in meagre numbers at single spots. Thus the spatial patterning of the artifactual material precludes the possibility of categorising most of the sites as settlements or base camps. At Raipalli, the collection is large but not enough to term it as a permanent settlement site. Only at Murtuzapoor are artifacts available in substantial numbers and the prolificacy may be attributed to the local availability of raw material. It was both a habitation and manufactory site.

The foregoing evidence seems to suggest that the Upper Palaeolithic and Mesolithic people wandered widely in the Manjra valley, camping at the same spots again and again. If the rich faunal evidences discovered elsewhere in the Manjra valley are an indication, lack of food resources was not the constraint, which forced them to habitual nomadism. Raw material resources however provide a part explanation. In the two seasons survey of the area, it was only at Chalki-Murtuzapoor that raw material sources were noticed. There are few gravel spreads either in the bed or on the banks of the river all along the course. Raw material nodules had to be imported from Upper reaches of the river where it cuts across the amygdaloid trap beds. This must have caused regular movements along the river course. But import of raw materials alone may not account for the entire range of movements.

As already stated, the undulating terrain of the countryside favoured lake formation which would retain water for a part of the year. In the dry season, the Manjra river alone was the water source to which animals and men thronged. The seasonal movements to and away from the river also need to be taken into consideration to account for the wide dispersal of artifactual occurrences.

Chapter - IV

UPPER-PALAEOLITHIC CULTURE

Two stone age cultures are represented in the Manjra valley. These are Upper Palaeolithic and Mesolithic. It is interesting to note that Lower and Middle Palaeolithic evidences are not observed at all in the valley.

There are seven sites where Upper Palaeolithic artifacts alone were discovered and at 30 others both Upper Palaeolithic and Microlithic artifacts were found together. The total number of Upper Palaeolithic finished tools is 217. These include blades, flakes, scrapers, borers, backed pieces and burins. The artifacts were made on flakes, blades and cores. The flake made artifacts account for 133 (61.29%), the blade made ones 76 (35.01%), where as the core made ones were 8 (3.7%). Thus it is clear that the flake element was predominant in the industry. Further, prepared core element occurs to the extent of 31.88% in the flakes and flake made tools. The Upper Palaeolithic industry of the Manjra valley may be characterised as 'Flake-Blade' industry. In addition to the finished tools, there are 82 blade, blanks, flake blanks and cores.

The raw material used was mainly chert (71%). Other raw-materials used were jasper (13.4%), agate (14%) and chalcedony (1.60%). These raw materials were available locally in the trap beds, cutting across which the Manjra river flows in the upper reaches of its course. The river must have picked up these silicious nodules, transported down stream and deposited them in its gravel bed. An exposure of the sandy gravel containing these varieties of cryptocrystaline silica is noticed near Chalki. It is understandable that the Upper Palaeolithic people picked up the raw materials from the gravel spreads. But at no other place was noticed an exposure of the gravel either on the bank or on the stream bed. Another source of raw material, available to the prehistoric man, was in the form of out crops observed at Murtuzapoor. The agate/chert bands exposed on the site bear chipping marks so that the material was flaked off for tool manufacture. At no place, other than Chalki-Murtuzapoor area, the raw material sources were observed. From this it appears that the raw material was neither plentiful nor available close at hand, at most of the sites explored.

The Upper Palaeolithic artifacts were manufactured by using different free flaking and controlled flaking techniques. The free flaking technique involved chipping out of nodules and blocks, flakes of convenient size for fashioning implements there on. The two techniques of controlled flaking, liberally employed, were the prepared core and the blade techniques. Prepared cores and flakes removed thereof are both present in the collection. But there are no blade cores where as the blade element in the total assemblage accounts for 35.01%. Therefore it has to be surmised that it was possible for the tool makers to remove long blade-like flakes from suitable cores with flat platforms. The flake blanks and blade blanks prepared by the above techniques were fashioned into finished forms by retouching the edges. Three types of retouching are generally observed. There are alternate retouch, steep retouch and back blunting. The tools categorised as (retouched) flakes, blades, and backed blades show alternate retouch. Steep retouching was done on various types of scrapers. Backblunting occurs on backed pieces. But not all backed pieces show blunting by retouch. There are several specimens with natural backs. Points show retouched lateral margins converging into a sharp point. There are only two specimens of tanged points, the others being simple ones some with thin bases. Borers have keen (needle like) points created by retouch either alround or half the circumference. The burins are single-blow-type ones with retouched opposite margins. Bold retouch is observed in some of the scrapers. But denticulates are not present in the collection.

The data concerning the artifact types is as follows:

1. SCRAPERS : These are 106 in number constituting 48.85% of the total number of finished tools. These are sub-divided as side, end, convex and hollow, taking the form of the working edge in to consideration. There are also some composite forms, like side cum end scrapers, side cum hollow scrapers and scraper cum borers.

	Side Scraper	End Scraper	Side cum end Scraper	Hollow Scraper	Convex Scraper
LENGTH RANGE in mm					
6-10	—	—	—	—	—
11-15	—	—	—	—	—
16-20	—	—	—	—	—
21-25	—	—	—	1	—
26-30	—	2	—	1	—
31-35	2	2	—	1	1
36-40	5	—	—	3	3
41-45	3	—	—	4	5
46-50	2	1	—	6	9
51-55	7	3	2	1	4
56-60	5	2	1	3	5
61-65	—	—	1	2	2
66-70	3	—	—	1	1
BREADTH RANGE in mm.					
16-20	—	1	—	—	—
21-25	2	1	—	—	—
26-30	9	—	2	6	3
31-35	6	1	2	4	8
36-40	4	4	—	3	6
41-45	4	3	—	5	5
46-50	1	—	—	5	4
51-55	—	—	—	—	4
56-60	1	—	—	—	—

THICKNESS RANGE in mm					
6-10	1	5	2	9	5
11-15	12	2	1	8	12
16-20	4	1	1	6	8
21-25	—	2	—	—	6

(a) Side Scrapers : These are twenty seven in number, 17 on flakes and 10 on blades. Their length, breadth and thickness ranges are 3.3 to 7.0 mm., 2.5 to 5.6 mm. and 0.7 to 1.8mm.

1. MZP - 26 : Side scraper on oval flake. Right margin shows steep retouching in upward direction. Dorsal surface uneven. Ventral surface plain.

Chert. (Fig. 4)

2. MZP - 28 : Side scraper on triangular flake. Right margin steeply retouched. Left margin thick and blunt.

Chert. (Fig. 4)

3. MZP - 22 : Side scraper on blade. Right margin shows steep retouch. Left margin unworked. Low ridge on dorsal surface. Ventral surface plain.

Chert. (Fig. 4)

4. RPL- 1 : Side scraper on thick blade. Right lateral margin shows steep retouch. Dorsal surface humped in the middle and prominently ridged along. Left margin irregular.

Chert. (Fig. 4 P1.4)

(b) End Scrapers : There are twelve end scrapers—eight on blade and four on flake. Length ranges from 26 to 70 mm., width range between 22 - 47 mm., and thickness range between 8 - 22 mm.

1. MZP -31 : End scraper on longish flake, wide in the lower half. Distal edge steeply retouched on to the ventral surface. Shallow irregular scars on the distal surface.

Chert. (Fig. 4 P1.4)

2. KPL - 6 : End scraper on thick bladelet. Distal end steeply retouched in upward direction from the ventral surface. Low parallel ridges on distal surface. Right margin thinner than the other.

Agate. (Fig. 4)

(c) **Side cum End Scrapers :** Seven specimens of this type are available, 3 each on flake and blade and 1 on core. These fall in length range between 54-64 mm., breadth range 26 - 33 mm., and thickness range 16 - 17 mm.

RPL - 26 : Side cum end scraper on thick blade, narrowing towards distal end. Right margin and the distal end steeply retouched from the ventral surface. Slightly water worn.

Agate. Fig. 4)

MZP - 48 : Side cum end scraper on thick triangular flake. Left lateral margin boldly retouched. One short and one long margin in the upward direction from the ventral surface.

Chert. (Fig. 4)

(d) Convex Scrapers : These constitute the largest number among the scraper variants with thirty two specimens, 28 on flake and 2 each on blade and core. These fall in length range between 37 - 67 mm., breadth range 24 - 54 mm., thickness range 8 - 24 mm.

MZP - 38 : Convex scraper on oval flake with wide convex edge steeply retouched in upward direction from the ventral surface.

Chert. (Fig. 4)

MZP - 37 : Convex scraper on blade. (Long flake?) with the side margins converging to widely rounded distal end. The convex margin shows steep upward retouch from ventral surface. Low forked ridge and shallow irregular scars on dorsal surface.

Chert. (Fig. 5)

(e) Hollow Scrapers : There are twenty four specimens, 19 of which were made on flake and 5 on blades. They fall in the length range between 28 - 67 mm., breadth range 28 - 50 mm., and thickness range 8 - 18 mm.

MZP - 44 : Hollow scraper on side struck flake with faceted platform. Hollow scraping edge steeply retouched in upward direction on the wide margin opposite the platform. Centrally directed flake scars on the dorsal surface.

Chert. (Fig. 5)

MZP - 45 : Hollow scraper on blade with pointed base. Hollow scraping edge steeply worked in upward direction in the upper half of the left lateral margin. Right margin crooked.

Chert. (Fig. 5)

MZP-46 : Double hollow scraper on oblong side struck flake. The hollow scraping edges worked by steep retouching one each on to dorsal and ventral surfaces.

(Fig. 5)

PKT - 5: Side-cum-hollow scraper on thick triangular flake with unequal margins. The margin opposite the platform is steeply retouched all along and the short right margin shows hollow scraping edge. The retouch on both the margins was done in upward direction from the dorsal surface. The dorsal surface shows low ridges.

Agate. (Fig. 5)

2. BORERS : This tool type is represented by nine numbers, 6 on flake, 1 on blade and 2 on core. The size ranges are as follows :

Length — 31 — 88 mm.
Breadth — 25 — 40 mm.
Thickness — 6 — 15 mm.

Size in mm.	length Range.	Breadth Range.	Thickness Range.
1 - 5	—	—	—
6 - 10	—	—	3

11 - 15	—	—	5
16 - 20	—	—	1
21 - 25	—	—	—
26 - 30	—	5	—
31 - 35	2	1	—
36 - 40	3	2	—
41 - 45	3	1	—
46 - 50	—	—	—
51 - 55	1	—	—

The illustrated specimens are described below :

PLG - 2 : Borer on flake with a stout needle like point with a fine retouch on either margin.

Jasper. (Fig. 5, Pl. 4)

MZP - 49 : Borer on blade, the side edges nearly parallel and retouched converge to a pointed projection at the distal end.

Jasper. (Fig. 5)

MZP - 53 : Borer on prepared core. Oval in shape with thin section. The lateral margin retouched all along and converge to a pointed projection. Centrally directed shallow flake scars on one surface and a prominent ridge on the other.

Chert. (Fig. 5)

(f) Scraper Cum Borers : This is a composite tool type, represented by four specimens, three on flake and one on core. They fall in the following size ranges :

Length — 27 — 58 mm.
Breadth — 17 — 38 mm.
Thickness — 6 — 19 mm.

Size in mm.	Length Range	Breadth Range	Thickness Range
1-5	—	—	—
5-10	—	—	2
11-15	—	—	2
16-20	—	2	—
21-25	—	—	—
26-30	—	2	—
31-35	—	—	—
36-40	2	—	—
41-45	2	—	—

MZP - 51 : Side scraper cum borer on thick end struck flake. Right margin steeply retouched all along in upward direction. The side margins meet at a keen point on the distal end. Jasper (Fig. 5 Pl. 4)

3. POINTS : These are eight in number, 5 on flakes and 3 on blades. Their length range is 36 - 75 mm., breadth range 26 - 45mm., and thickness range 11 to 25 mm. are as follows :

Size in mm.	Length Range	Breadth Range	Thickness Range
11-15	—	—	4
16-20	—	—	3
21- 25	—	—	1
26-30	—	3	—
31-35	—	—	—
36-40	3	3	—
41-45	—	2	—
46-50	3	—	—
51-55	—	—	—
56-60	—	—	—

61-65	1	—	—
66-70	—	—	—
71-75	1	—	—

RPD-2 : Point on prepared flake of triangular shape. The lateral retouched margins meet at pointed tip. The base was thinned by removing a flake on dorsal surface.

Chert. (Fig. 6, Pl.4)

RPL-44: Small specimen of point on end struck flake. The left lateral margin shows retouch and inclines to meet the other at pointed tip. Prominent ridge on dorsal surface.

Jasper. (Fig.6 Pl.4)

MZP-67 : Tanged point on blade with a retouched side margin converging at a pointed tip. There is a notch at the base of the left margin to make incipient tang. Single shouldered point.

Jasper (Fig.6)

4. BURINS : There are nine specimens of this tool type, 3 on flakes, 4 on blades and 2 on cores. The size ranges are :

Length — 33 —57 mm.
Breadth — 22 —43 mm.
Thickness — 9 —16 mm.

Size in mm.	Length Range	Breadth Range	Thickness Range
6-10	—	—	2
11-15	—	—	5
16-20	—	—	2
21-25	—	2	—
26-30	—	2	—
31-35	2	2	—
36-40	2	2	—

41-45	2	1	—
46-50	1	—	—
51-55	1	—	—
56-60	1	—	—

Two Illustrated specimens are described below:

PPD-22: Angle burin on tabular core of oval shape. Left margin thicker than the right. Right margin retouched at the upper end. Burin spall at the upper end of the left lateral margin.

Chert. (Fig. 6 Pl.4)

DTB - 2: Bec-de-flute-blow type burin on short blade, pointed at the distal end. Two spalls at the distal end on to either margin meet at acute angle. Prominent ridge on dorsal surface.

Quartz. (Fig. 6 Pl.4)

5. BACKED PIECES: These are thirty seven in number, 16 made on flakes and 21 made on blades. Their size ranges are —

Length —29 —66 mm.
Breadth —18 —60 mm.
Thickness — 7 —39 mm.

Size in mm.	Length Range	Breadth Range	Thickness Range
6-10	—	—	15
11-15	—	—	16
16-20	—	8	4
21-25	—	8	1
26-30	2	8	—
31-35	—	7	—
36-40	6	4	1
41-45	15	—	—
46-50	4	1	—

51-55	2	—	—
56-60	1	—	—
61-65	6	—	—
66-70	1	—	—

MZP-62: Crescentic backed piece on side struck flake. Left margin thicker and blunted by retouch. Right margin shows fine alternate retouch.

Chert (Fig. 6 Pl. 4)

RPL-38: Backed piece on blade with left margin straight and blunt and the right slightly convex and showing used marks.

Jasper (Fig. 6)

MZP-64: Backed piece on bladelets of triangular section and parallel sides. The thicker margin naturally blunt and covered with cortex. The thinner margin shows fine retouch.

Jasper (Fig. 6)

RPD-4: Backed piece on broken blade with one margin thicker than the other. The blunt back partly retouched and partly natural. The working edge shows clear used marks.

Opal (Fig. 6)

6. BLADES: Parallel or nearly parallel sided end struck flakes with clear evidences of retouch on one or both the margins are considered under the head of blades. There are twenty three of this type in the collection. These are of widely varying size and fall in the size range.

Length — 21 — 71 mm.
Breadth — 18 — 51 mm.
Thickness — 4 — 18 mm.

Size in mm.	Length Range	Breadth Range	Thickness Range
1-5	—	—	2
6-10	—	—	4
11-15	—	—	10
16-20	—	1	2
21-25	—	4	—
26-30	—	2	—
31-35	2	3	—
36-40	3	8	—
41-45	3	—	—
46-50	2	—	—
51-55	3	1	—
56-60	1	—	—
61-65	3	—	—
66-70	4	—	—
71-75	1	—	—

MZP-60: Parallel sided blade broken at the distal end. Prominent ridge on dorsal surface. Right margin shows fine retouch.

Agate. (Fig. 7 Pl.5)

BRP-12 : Full length blade with parallel sides and pointed distal end. Prominent ridge on dorsal surface. Fine retouch along the right margin.

Jasper. (Fig. 7)

DTB-1: Full length blade narrowing towards distal end. Right margin shows fine retouch all along. Nibbled chipping on the left margin. Prominent ridge on dorsal surface.

Chert. (Fig. 7 Pl.4)

MZP-110 : Complete specimen of blade of triangular form.

Retouch on both the margins. Shallow blade scars on dorsal surface.

Chert. (Fig. 7 Pl.5)

7. FLAKES: Flakes of different sizes and shapes with retouch on at least a part of the edge are grouped under this category. Their size ranges are :-

Length —37 — 64 mm.

Breadth — 23 — 50 mm.

Thickness — 8 — 20 mm.

Size in mm.	Length Range	Breadth Range	Thickness Range
6-10	—	—	4
11-15	—	—	13
16-20	—	—	9
21-25	—	2	—
26-30	—	3	—
31-35	1	1	—
36-40	3	8	—
41-45	3	5	—
46-50	8	4	—
51-55	2	1	—
56-60	3	1	—
61-65	4	—	—
66-70	1	—	—

The selected specimens are described below :

MZP-9: Flake of trapezoid shape with fine retouch on the ventral surface all along the margin except at the platform.

Chert. (Fig.7)

GTP-9: Thick oblong flake with retouched side margins. Prominent ridges on dorsal surface. Ventral surface shows shallow scars and low ridge.

Agate (Fig. 7)

BRP-3 : Oval flake of thick section with fine alternate retouch all along the margin. Ventral and dorsal surfaces plain. Platform prepared.

Chert. (Fig. 7)

GRK-6: Side struck flake with straight right margin and irregular left margin. Prominent ridge on dorsal surface. Fine retouch on the right margin.

Chert. (Fig. 7)

OTHERS :

Blade Blanks : These are blade like flakes without retouch. Twenty four specimens of this type are present in this collection. The size ranges:

Length — 28 — 60 mm.
Breadth — 18 — 52 mm.
Thickness — 6 — 18 mm.

Size in mm	Length Range	Breadth Range	Thickness Range
6-10	—	—	14
11-15	—	—	9
16-20	—	3	1
21-25	—	5	—
26-30	3	4	—
31-35	5	10	—
36-40	3	1	—
41-45	8	1	—
46-50	4	—	—
51-55	1	—	—

GTR-10: Blade blank, complete specimen with the two sides slightly convex. Shallow scar on the dorsal surface. Section thin. Agate.

(Fig. 7 Pl.5)

PLG-9 : Blade blank with convex sides and pointed tip. Dorsal surface partly plain and partly covered with shallow scars. Opal

(Fig. 8 Pl.5)

Flake Blanks : All flakes without retouching of edges are grouped under this head. There are forty five flake blanks in the collection. The size ranges are:

Length —29 —70 mm.
Breadth —25 —58 mm.
Thickness —6 —23 mm.

Size in mm.	Length Range	Breadth Range	Thickness Range
6-10	—	—	12
11-15	—	—	17
16-20	—	—	10
21-25	—	5	3
26-30	1	3	3
31-35	4	8	—
36-40	10	5	—
41-45	12	9	—
46-50	4	6	—
51-55	2	4	—
56-60	2	3	—
61-65	4	1	—
66-70	6	1	—

KDB-4: Flake blank of oval shape, with faceted platform. Two centrally directed shallow scars on the left upper margin. Ventral surface plain.

Chert. (Fig. 8)

MTR-8: Oval specimen of flake blank with thin section. Platform prepared. Shallow steeped scars on the dorsal surface. Ventral surface plain.

Agate. (Fig. 8)

MZP-84 : Long end struck flake with prominent ridge on dorsal surface. Ventral surface plain. Distal end rounded.

Jasper. (Fig. 8)

MZP-99 : Oval specimen of flake blank from prepared core. Shallow longitudinal scar on dorsal surface. Platform faceted. Bulb of percussion diffused.

Jasper. (Fig. 8)

MZP-100 : Oval flake with prepared platform and convergent scars on dorsal surface. Ventral surface plain.

Chert. (Fig. 8 Pl.5)

Amorphous Cores : Cores of irregular shape and size are present in the collection. There are eleven specimens of this type. The size ranges are :

Length — 38 — 77 mm.
Breadth — 15 — 58 mm.
Thickness — 14 — 33 mm.

Size in mm.	Length Range	Breadth Range	Thickness Range
16-20	—	—	2
21-25	—	—	2
26-30	—	—	5
31-35	—	5	2

36-40	—	—	—
41-45	—	4	—
46-50	5	–	—
51-55	3	2	—
56-60	1	—	—
61-65	2	—	—

Prepared Cores : There are two specimens of prepared cores. These are generally flatish and show faceted platforms. Both the specimens are illustrated.

Size in mm.	Length Range	Breadth Range	Thickness Range
20-25	—	—	1
26-30	—	—	—
31-35	—	—	—
36-40	—	—	—
41-45	—	—	1
46-50	—	—	—
51-55	—	1	—
56-60	—	—	—
61-65	2	1	—

MZP-76 : Prepared core with faceted platform and convergent scars on the surface.

Chert. (Fig. 8)

MZP-77 : Tabular core of oval form with platform worked with centrally directed shallow scars on the surface. The rear surface is plain except for some deep marginal scars .Flake Core.

Chert. (Fig. 8 Pl.5)

UPPER PALAEOLITHIC ARTIFACTS

1. SCRAPERS	... ...	106	48.85%
(a) Side scrapers (Fl 17+Bl 10)	27	25.47%	
(b) End scrapers (Fl 4+Bl 8)	12	11.32%	
(c) Side cum end scrapers (Cr 1+ (Fl 3 + Bl 3)	7	6.60%	
(d) Convex scrapers (Fl 28+Bl 4)	32	30.19%	
(e) Hollow scraper (Fl 19+Bl 5)	24	22.64%	
(f) Scraper cum borers (Fl 3 + Bl 1)	4	3.78%	
2. BORERS (Fl 6+Bl 1+Cr.2) ...	9	4.15%	
3. POINTS (Fl 5+Bl 3) ...	8	3.69%	
4. BURINS (Fl 3 + Bl 4+Cr. 2) ...	9	4.15%	
5. BACKED PIECES (Fl 16+Bl 21) ...	37	17.05%	
6. BLADES ...	23	10.59%	
7. FLAKES ...	25	11.52%	
Total :	217		

OTHERS

Blade Blanks	—	24
Flake Blanks	—	45
Ordinary cores	—	11
Prepared cores	—	2
Flake made	133	61.29%
Blade made	76	35.01%
Core made	8	3.70%
	217	

Chapter - V

MESOLITHIC CULTURE

Mesolithic industries are discovered at 30 sites. At three sites they are found alone, and at 27 sites they occur along with Upper Palaeolithic industries. The distribution pattern of the Mesolithic sites leads to two possible inferences - 1. foraging operations of the Upper Palaeolithic and Mesolithic people were more or less similar, requiring the same spots to be repeatedly visited; 2. there may not have been a chronological gap between the two industries.

As pointed out with reference to the Upper Palaeolithic industries, the microliths too occur in twos and threes at most of the sites. Only one site i.e., Raipalli yielded the artifacts in sizeable numbers (74). Most of the implements were made on chert (81.33%). However we find supplementation of other raw materials to a small extent (agate 16.33% and jasper 2.34%). Just as the Upper Palaeolithic men had, the Microlithic makers too faced the problem of non-availability of raw material and they had to import the raw material from the Upper reaches of Manjra.

None of the Mesolithic sites yielded geometric forms and thus, the Mesolithic culture of the Manjra valley may be categorised as aceramic and non-geometric.

Microlithic artifacts were made by employing different free flaking and controlled flaking techniques as in the Upper Palaeolithic times of this valley. But fluted cores occur more in number indicating the use of blade technique to a greater extent. In the assemblage of finished tools, the blade made ones account for 32.56%. Besides these, there are 17 blade blanks and 23 fluted cores. In the total collection of finished tool specimens numbering 150, their percentage is 47.33. It may be noted that bladelets, more than the full length blades, were preferred for fashioning the tools.

The Mesolithic industries of the Manjra Valley were to a large extent based on the production of flake blanks and flake made tools. The flake blanks and the flake made tools together are 71 in number constituting 56.67% of the total number of specimens collected.

The Microlithic tools include a variety of finished artifacts; scrapers of different types, backed pieces, borers, scraper cum borers, blades, flakes and burins. The non-artifacts comprise blade blanks (17), flake blanks (21), amorphous and fluted cores (23).

1. SCRAPERS : These comprise 33 specimens constituting 38.15% of the finished artifacts. Scrapers include the side, end, side-cum-end, convex, hollow and transverse. The length, breadth and thickness size ranges of the scrapers are given below:

	Side Scraper	Side cum end Scraper	Convex Scraper	Hollow Scraper
LENGTH RANGE in mm.				
21-25	—	—	—	1
26-30	4	—	1	1
31-35	—	—	2	8
36-40	8	1	1	—
41-45	4	—	—	—
BREADTH RANGE in mm.				
11-15	1	—	—	—
16-20	1	—	—	1
21-25	2	—	1	6
26-30	5	—	2	—
31-35	7	1	1	4

THICKNESS RANGE in mm.				
1-5	—	—	—	1
6-10	11	—	2	7
11-15	5	1	1	3
16-20	—	—	1	—
21-25	—	—	—	—
26-30	—	—	—	—
31-35	—	—	—	—

(a) Side Scrapers : There are seventeen side scrapers, 6 on flake and 11 on blade. These fall in size ranges :

Length	— 30	— 45 mm.
Breadth	— 15	— 33 mm. and
Thickness	— 7	— 12 mm.

The illustrated specimens are described below:

RCM-5 : Side scraper on thick blade with steeply retouched margin. The opposite margin is blunted. The distal surface shows prominent ridge. Ventral surface plain. Slightly water worn.

Chert. (Fig. 9 Pl.5)

RPL-4 : Side scraper on thick blade. The left margin steeply retouched on to the dorsal surface which shows deep scars and central ridge. Ventral surface plain. Right margin thick and crooked.

Chert. (Fig. 9)

RPL-9: Side scraper on oval flake. Gradually thinning from the right to the left margin. The latter steeply retouched in upward direction from ventral surface. The dorsal surface shows deep negative scar.

Chert (Fig. 9)

RPL-7 : Side scraper on trapezoidal flake with left margin steeply retouched. The specimen broken at the two ends. Low double ridge and deep scar with clear ripple marks on dorsal surface.

Agate. (Fig. 9)

(b) End Scrapers : —

(c) Side cum end Scrapers : Only one specimen of this type is available. Its dimensions are 40 x 35 x 13 mm.

DKP-5 : Side cum end scraper on sub-triangular flake with the right margin and the lower end steeply worked for scraping edge. Deep central scar on dorsal surface.

Opal. (Fig. 9 Pl. 5)

(d) Convex Scrapers : This type is represented by four specimens (12.12% in scrapers), I on blade and 3 on flake. The size ranges are as follows:

Length — 35 — 44 mm.
Breadth — 25 — 33 mm., and
Thickness — 9 — 18 mm.

PKT-4 : Convex scraper on thick blade with right margin straight and the left convex. The latter shows steep retouch partially on to either surface. Deep scar on dorsal surface.

Chert. (Fig. 9)

RPL-23 : Convex scraper on thick oval flake. Convexed, boldly retouched margin. Reworked specimen. Ventral surface plain. Prominent 'Y' ridge on dorsal surface.

Chert. (Fig. 9)

RPL-25 : Double edged scraper on thick longitudinal flake. Left margin convex and steeply retouched in upward direction. Right margin shows bold chipping. Twin ridged dorsal surface. Ventral surface plain.

Chert. (Fig. 9)

(e) Hollow scrapers : Eleven specimens of this type (33.3%) are available, 5 on blade and 6 on flake. The size ranges of the flake made ones :

Length — 30 — 45 mm.
Breadth — 20 — 35 mm., and

Thickness — 6 — 10 mm.

The blade made ones fall in :

Length — 33 — 50 mm.,

Breadth — 21 — 34 mm., and

Thickness — 7 — 14 mm.

RPL-14 : Hollow scraper on flake of irregular form. Hollow scraping edge produced by retouching the right margin. Both the surfaces are plain. Specimen slightly rolled.

Chert. (Fig. 9 Pl.5)

RPL-15 : Hollow scraper on thick flake with prominent bulb on the ventral surface and hollow scraping edge on the right margin. Multidirectional ridges on the dorsal surface.

Chert. (Fig. 9 Pl.5)

BDG-6 : Hollow scraper on thick blade, prominent ridge on dorsal surface. (Core rejuvenation flake). Hollow scraping edge on to ventral surface on the right margin.

Opal. (Fig. 9 Pl.5)

RPL-10 : Hollow scraper on wide blade with left margin straight and the right margin slightly convex. Hollow scraping edge at the distal end. Dorsal surface shows low ridge.

Chert. (Fig. 9 Pl.5)

RPD-2 : Small specimen of hollow scraper on thick blade. Left margin shows double hollow scraping edge. Prominent ridge on the dorsal surface. Ventral surface plain.

Jasper. (Fig. 10)

2. BORERS : The borer type is represented by thirteen specimens constituting 15.12% of the finished tools. Of them 10 are made on flake and 3 on blade. The size ranges of the flake made ones are :

Length — 26 — 38 mm.

Breadth — 20 — 32 mm., and

Thickness - 6 — 14 mm.

The size range of the blade made ones :

Length — 28 — 32 mm.,

Breadth — 20 — 30 mm., and

Thickness — 6 — 8 mm.

Table showing the size ranges of Borers

Size in mm.	Length	Breadth	Thickness
1-5	—	—	1
6-10	—	—	9
11-15	—	—	3
16-20	—	3	—
21-25	—	2	—
26-30	5	5	—
31-35	5	3	—
36-40	3	—	—

Four illustrated specimens are described below:

RPL-31 : Borer on flake. A stout needle like point created by retouching the sides. Dorsal surface shows a low ridge along the opposite margin.

Chert. (Fig. 10 Pl.5)

SRD-1 : Borer on oval flake with the right margin retouched for borer point. Left margin convex. Shallow flake scars on dorsal surface.

Chert. (Fig. 10)

RPL-28 : Borer on short blade with oblique distal end and a forked ridge on dorsal surface. Right margin prolonged and retouched to a keen point. Specimen slightly water-worn.

Chert. (Fig. 10)

RCM-3 : Borer on blade with a deep dent on the right margin. The distal end is retouched for stout borer point.

Chert. (Fig. 10)

3. SCRAPER CUM BORERS : There are four specimens of this composite tool type constituting 4.65%. These specimens fall in:

Length — 25 — 38 mm.
Breadth — 20 — 30 mm., and
Thickness — 5 — 10 mm.

One illustrated specimen is described below.

HNP-7 : Scraper cum borer on quadrangular side struck flake. The long margin opposite the platform shows steep retouch all along. The left margin shows borer point. A prominent ridge across the dorsal surface.

Chert. (Fig. 10)

Table showing the size ranges of Scraper cum Borer

Size in mm.	Length	Breadth	Thickness
1—5	—	—	2
6—10	—	—	2
11—15	—	—	—
16—20	—	2	—
21—25	1	1	—
26—30	1	1	—
31—35	—	—	—
36—40	2	—	—

4. POINTS : There are three specimens of points, all made on blade. Its percentage in the finished tools is 3.48.

The size ranges are :

Length — 37 — 39 mm.
Breadth — 25 — 33 mm.
Thickness — 5 — 10 mm.

Table showing the size ranges of Points

Size in mm.	Length	Breadth	Thickness
1—5	—	—	1
6—10	—	—	2
11—15	—	—	—
16—20	—	—	—
21—25	—	1	—
26—30	—	1	—
31—35	—	1	—
36—40	3	—	—

MTR-1 : Point on blade with two side edges meeting at pointed end. The base is traingular and shows incipient tang. A low ridge, a deep scar on dorsal surface.

Chert. (Fig. 10 Pl.5)

GTP-5 : Point on thick blade. The side edges convex and retouched to meet at pointed end. Tip broken. Prominent ridge and cortex for half the portion on dorsal surface.

Chert. (Fig. 10)

5. BURINS : There is only one specimen of this type, made on blade. Its dimensions are 43 x 25 x 11 mm.

RPL-32 : Burin on thick blade with prominent forked ridge on dorsal surface. The distal end shows two spalls cut into the opposite margin and meeting each other at low angle.

Chert. (Fig. 10)

6. BACKED PIECES : There are twenty one specimens, 13 made on flake, 5 on blade and 3 on core. Its percentage in the finished tools is 24.40. The size ranges of the flake made ones are :

Length — 25 — 42 mm.

Breadth — 12 — 35 mm., and

Thickness — 4 — 12 mm.

On the blade made ones :

Length — 30 — 42 mm.,

Breadth — 22 — 30 mm., and

Thickness — 10 — 13 mm.

And on the core made ones :

Length — 28 — 46 mm.,

Breadth — 18 — 25 mm., and

Thickness — 6 — 15 mm.

Table showing the size ranges of Backed Pieces

Size in mm.	Length	Breadth	Thickness
1—5	—	—	5
6—10	—	—	11
11—15	—	2	5
16—20	—	4	—
21—25	2	11	—
26—30	7	2	—
36—40	5	—	—
41—45	3	—	—
46—50	1	—	—

The following illustrated specimens are described.

DKP-3 : Backed piece on long flake of trapezoid form with three shorter margins blunted by retouch. The long opposite margin shows bold chipping.

Chert. (Fig. 10)

RPL-63 : Backed piece on small flake thinning from the left to the right margin. Fragment of a fluted core. The left margin shows fine retouch.

Agate. (Fig. 10)

RPL-40 : Backed piece on broken blade. Left margin blunted by retouch. Right margin thick and shows pointed retouch.

Chert. (Fig. 10)

RPD-3 : Backed piece on blade. Right margin thick and blunt. The left shows fine retouch. Shallow scar on distal surface.

Chert. (Fig. 11)

HPR-4 : Crescentic backed piece on blade. The curved margin thick and blunt. The opposite straight one shows used marks. Two blade scars on dorsal surface.

Chert. (Fig. 11)

BLR-3 : Reject fluted core turned as backed piece. The right margin thick and blunt and the left margin slightly convex and alternately retouched all along.

Opal. (Fig. 11)

7. BLADES : This tool type is represented by seven specimens comprising 8.13% of the finished tools. Their size ranges are :

Length — 25 — 42 mm.,
Breadth — 13 — 26 mm., and
Thickness — 4 — 10 mm.

Table showing the size ranges of blades

Size in mm.	Length	Breadth	Thickness
1—5	—	—	2
6—10	—	—	5
11—15	—	2	—
16—20	—	—	—
21—25	1	4	—
26—30	—	1	—

31—35	2	—	—
36—40	2	—	—
41—45	2	—	—

The illustrated specimens are described below :

RPL-34 : Blade broken. Prominent ridge on dorsal surface. Left margin retouched all along. Used marks on right margin.
Chert. (Fig. 11)

RPL-83 : Blade broken at either end. Left margin finely retouched. Right plain. Shallow multiple flake scars on dorsal surface.
Chert. (Fig. 11 Pl. 5)

8. FLAKES : This type is represented by four specimens (4.65%) in the finished tools collected. The size ranges are :

Length range — 22 — 32 m.,
Breadth range — 20 — 28 mm.,
Thickness range — 5 — 10 mm.

Table showing the size ranges of flakes

Size in mm.	Length	Breadth	Thickness
1—5	—	—	4
6—10	—	—	—
11—15	—	2	—
16—20	—	2	—
21—25	—	—	—
26—30	3	—	—
31—35	1	—	—
36—40	—	—	—
41—45	—	—	—

The description of the two illustrated specimens :

HPR-8 : Oval flake with faceted platform. Right margin finely retouched. Left margin has dent. Longitudinal ridge on dorsal surface.

Chert. (Fig. 11)

KSM-6 : Trapezoid flake with faceted platform with multiridged dorsal surface. Nibbled retouch on the margin.

Chert. (Fig. 11)

OTHERS :

1. BLADE BLANKS : Seventeen specimens of this type are present in the collection. The size ranges :

Length range — 25 — 40 mm.
Breadth range — 12 — 28 mm.
Thickness range — 3 — 12 mm.

Table showing the size ranges of blade blanks

Size of blade Blanks in mm.	Length	Breadth	Thickness
1—5	—	—	2
6—10	—	—	14
11—15	—	4	1
16—20	—	2	—
21—25	2	7	—
26—30	1	4	—
31—35	8	—	—
36—40	6	—	—

RPL-68 : Blade blank, broken. Right margin slightly convex. Left margin straight. Prominent ridge on dorsal surface. Ventral plain.

Agate. (Fig. 11 Pl. 5)

KSM-3 : Blade blank with double ridged dorsal surface. Left margin slightly concave and the right straight.

Chert. (Fig. 11)

2. FLAKE BLANKS : There are twenty one specimens in the collection. The size ranges fall in:

Length range — 22 — 40 mm.,
Breadth range — 5 — 34 mm., and
Thickness range — 3 — 18 mm.

Table showing the size ranges of flake blanks

Size in mm.	Length	Breadth	Thickness
1—5	—	—	6
6—10	—	—	12
11—15	—	2	3
16—20	—	5	—
21—25	3	4	—
26—30	6	7	—
31—35	9	3	—
36—40	3	—	—

GRK-1 : Pointed flake, end struck, Lateral margins widely curved. Low ridge and a scar on dorsal surface.

Agate. (Fig. 11)

CLK-4 : End struck flake, broken, prominent ridge on dorsal surface. Right margin thick and blunt.

Chert. (Fig. 11)

3. FLUTED (BLADE) CORES : There are twenty three specimens in the collection. The size ranges are :

Length range — 25 — 50 mm.,

Breadth range — 15 — 38 mm.,
Thickness range — 5 — 25 mm.

Table Showing The Size Ranges Of Fluted Cores

Size in mm.	Length	Breadth	Thickness
1—5	—	—	1
6—10	—	—	6
11—15	—	4	6
16—20	—	5	7
21—25	1	6	3
26—30	8	4	—
31—35	5	2	—
36—40	7	1	—
41—45	1	—	—
46—50	1	—	—

ATL-2 : Cylindrical blade core with flutations on the frontal face. Four flutations are fairly visible. The rear surface alternately chipped across leaving crested ridge like formation.

Jasper (Fig. 12 Pl. 5)

ATL-1 : Cylindrical fluted core with 'D' shaped section. The convex frontal part shows flutations. The rear flake surface covered with cortex.

Agate. (Fig. 12)

RPL-61 : Prismatic fluted core with a transverse scar forming the platform. Series of flutations on the rounded face. Rear flat surface covered with cortex.

Agate. (Fig. 12)

KDB-1 : Irregular multifaceted core with irregular flutations.

Chert. (Fig. 12)

4. ORDINARY CORES : There are three specimens of this type. Not illustrated.

MICROLITHIS ARTFACTS

1. SCRAPERS	33		38.14%
(a) Side scrapers (6Fl. + 11Bl.)	17 (51.5%)		
(b) End scraper	—		
(c) Side-cum-end scrapers (on blade)	1(3.07%)		
(d) Convex scraper (3Fl.+1Bl.)	4(12.12%)		
(e) Hollow scrapers (6F.+5B.)	11(33.3%)		
2. BORERS (10 Fl. + 3 Bl.)		13	15.12%
3. SCRAPER CUM BORERS (4.Fl) ...		4	4.65%
4. POINTS (Bl.) ...		3	3.48%
5. BURINS (Bl.) ...		1	1.43%
6. BACKED PIECES (13F+5B+3C)		21	24.40%
7. BLADES ...		7	8.13%
8. FLAKES ...		4	4.65%
Total		86	
OTHERS			
1. Blade blanks ...		17	
2. Flake blanks ...		21	
3. Fluted cores ...		23	
4. Ordinary Cores ...		3	
		64	
Rejects ...		128	
Flake made tools	55		
Blade made tools	28		
Core made tools	3		

Chapter - VI

DISCUSSION AND DATA COMPARISON

The foregoing chapters have shown that the Manjra valley produced evidences of Upper Palaeolithic and Mesolithic cultures. The evidences are available in the form of surface occurrences of artifactual materials at 40 localities. Thirty of the sites furnished evidence of both the cultures, where as seven others are exlusively Upper Palaeolithic and three exclusively Mesolithic. It has been indicated that the two cultures followed one another without much of a chronological break.

The statigraphy of the Manjra sedimentary deposits is simple. The river preserved two terraces, the first being a constructional terrace and the second an erosional step. The river Manjra now flows through a deeply entrenched valley exposing on the sites bed-rock at varying heights. This clearly indicates stream rejuvenation. It has been postulated that the severe cutting down of the bed level preceded the presence of Upper Palaeolithic man in the area.

The river Manjra is a part of the Godavari system and as such should more or less faithfully reflect the fluctuations in the course of the latter. Stream rejuvenation from + 20 to -15 in relation to the present bed level has been observed in the upper reaches of Godavari and the tributary streams joining there at (IAR 1975-76 PP. 34, 35). The stream rejuvenation was accounted for epeirogenic movements of pleistocene date (Rajaguru, S.N. and Hegde, K.T.N. 1972). Geomorphic evidences for the same such as knick points, rock-cut benches etc., occur not only in Godavari but in a host of other streams, such as Narmada (Wainwright, G.A. 1968, Allchin and Hegde 1968); Tapti (Sali 1970) and Krishna. Though it is realised that the Deccan Plateau is seismically not so stable as imagined, the data concerning the neotectonics is inadequate for purposes of precise correlations.

The higher terrace of the Manjra valley is made up of sandy-pebbly gravel overlain by brownish silt and the latter in turn was succeeded by dark-brown soil (black-cotton soil). The terrace-1 deposits of the Manjra river should be equated with the second group of Narmada river (De Terra, H. and Paterson, T.T. 1939) and a part of the older fill of the upper Godavari and the Pravara (IAR 1955-56).

The sandy pebbly gravel can be equated with the middle Palaeolithic bearing gravels of the upper reaches of Godavari (Sankalia, H.D. 1964). Khan dated the lower group of Narmada between 1,20,000 and 6,000 years B.P. (Khan, E. 1968). A clear disconformity of unknown duration separates the lower and the upper groups of Narmada. Carbon 14 dates available for the Middle Palaeolithic range between 40,000 and 20,000 B.P. (Dhomdam, river

Krishna 39,590 + 9,200; Mula dam 31,076 + 5,550.
- 4,250 - 3,245

Ratikarar 31,750 + 1,820; Inamgaon, Ghod river 21,725 + 630
- 1,625 - 585,

Somnath 19,480 + 619 ; Paithan, Godavari river 19,025 ± 660,
- 560

Belan 17,765 ± 340).

The terrace-1 deposits of the Manjra river should more or less belong to the same time bracket. But no where are middle Palaeolithic tools available, in the presently explored segment of the Manjra valley. The reasons for the absence are not easy to furnish. The first evidences of human occupation of the area by the Upper Palaeolithic folk date to 20000 B.P. or there abouts. The Upper Palaeolithic artifacts, as already shown, occur on the surface of black soil which is an ubiquitous phenomenon in the area. The black soil is alkaline and contains caliches. A few lateritic pellets, also found on the surface, only indicate superficial drifts due to natural agencies. But a radio metric date for black-cotton soil in the lower Narmada gave a surprisingly recent date, 7000 B.P. (Rajaguru S.N., Hegde, K.T.M. 1972). The dated materials were caliches nodules from B/C. horizon. This need not cause concern because caliches can be of a later date than the formation of the black soil and as Hegde has shown black-cotton soils from different areas may not be of the same date (Hegde, K.T.M. 1972).

It is risky to draw inferences of palaeo climates from alluvial deposits of rivers. Fluvial activity depends on both climate and local geomorphic phenomenon. Sandy pebbly gravels or sandy gravels are being noticed in the upper courses of a number of peninsular streams. Some of these are found to be cross bedded. Sandy pebbly gravels are channel deposits of braided streams with an amount of turbulence of water flow. Torrential streams with braided courses are witnessed even today and therefore the sandy pebbly gravels do not indicate any significant difference of climate from the present.

The silty sands and silty clays which we commonly come across in the peninsular streams sometimes exhibit good lamination and gentle depositional dip. Raikes (Raikes, R. 1967) suggested low energy conditions for their formation. But according to Finzi (Vita-Finzi 1971) massive deposits of poorly sorted sandy silts moderately rich in clay content would suggest flash floods. Finer sediments may not always suggest lessening of the carrying capacity of the river. The volume of load remaining the same, there would be an impeded water flow due to choking up of the channel courses. Under these conditions, the rivers would fast upgrade the beds. It has been shown above, that the Manjra river experiences excessive floods at short intervals and the latest such recorded was in 1983.

The top member of the cliff sections viz., black-cotton soil is plastic, with high percentage of clay and humus. It was believed to have formed under the influence of protective cover of vegetation such as wooded forest. These soils are alkaline and consist of a variable percentage of caliche nodules suggesting a condition of aridity and lowering of sub-soil water tables. It is the author's conviction that the calcium concretions should be of a time subsequent to the formation of the black-cotton soil. According to Flint these secondary carbonates are well developed in areas receiving precipitation in the range of 500 mm. (Flint, R.F. 1963). In rain fall regimes of 800-500 mm. caliche nodules are found to frequently occur. Where the precipitation is less than 500 mm., massive calcrates seem to form. The region under study receives 896.7 mm. of rain per annum. But the rain fall records over the past 50 years show variation between 600 and 1100 mm. Thus, crystallization of calcium carbonate can take place in the area under the present conditions.

From the above observations, it should be clear that streams can deposit sandy pebbly gravels, sandy clayey silts and black earths all at the same time under climatic conditions presently obtaining in the area today. By clay mineral analysis Rajaguru has shown that the semi arid parts of the peninsular India such as the presently explored zone did not receive precipitation exceeding 750-1000 mm., in the late pleistocene period (Rajaguru, S.N. 1973).

As already shown, the Manjra valley is rich in faunal remains. The fauna recovered in the upper reaches of the river course in Maharashtra and Karnataka include Bubalus bubalis (Buffalo), Cervus sp (Deer), Equus Namadicus (Horse), Bos namadicus (Cattle), Elephas and Hippopotamus (IAR 1975-76). The fossil evidence indicated wood land-savannah type vegetation with patches of marsh in low lands. But the mammalian species represented are of a highly general kind with a wide range of distribution both in space and time. These are not the index types to help more precise climatic estimates.

UPPER PALAEOLITHIC CULTURE

The Upper Palaeolithic as a separate cultural phase in Indian prehistory has been recognised (Sankalia 1974; Thaper 1975-76) as a result of researches spread over the last 20 years **ANDHRA PRADESH**: (R.B. and H.B. Foote in 1844; Cammiade and Burkitt 1930; Soundara Rajan 1958; Isaac, N. 1960; S.N. Rao 1966; M.L.K. Murthy 1968, 1974, 1979; Timma Reddi 1970; M.L.K. Murthy & Timma Reddi 1976 and Kasturibai 1982); **MADRAS** : (K.V. Raman 1960-61; Vidula Jaiswal); **KARNATAKA** : (B. Subba

Rao 1963; Seshadri 1964; Paddaiah 1970; Pappu 1972); **MAHARASHTRA** : (K.R.V. Todd; Malik 1956; Corvinus 1960; Sankalia 1956, 1974; S.A.Sali 1973-74; R.V. Joshi and team 1975-76; Srinivasan); **GUJARAT** : (Allchin & Goudia 1971- 1972); **RAJASTHAN** : (Bridgit Allchin 1972); **MADHYA PRADESH** : (Wakankar 1957, Misra 1977); **UTTAR PRADESH** : (G.R. Sarma 1956-57, 1975); **BIHAR** : (A.K. Ghosh 1965-66, 1970) and **ASSAM:** (Sarma 1974). Upper Palaeolithic sites are now known to spread widely in the country (Fig. 13) from Ganga basin in the north to Tamilnadu in the South and from Assam in the east to Gujarat-Rajastan in the west. There are broad typo-technological similarities among these disparate groups of assemblages so that they may all be brought under one head, the Upper Palaeolithic. The available carbon 14 dates indicate that the upper Palaeolithic cultures flourished in India from about 20,000 to 10,000 years ago (Patne 1979-80 Asla). Within this time bracket, the industries must have evolved. The evolution of the industries in reference to the time scale as well as the regional variations noticeable in artifactual compositions make the Upper Palaeolithic a complex and fascinating area of study.

Dr. Sankalia (1974 PPIP p. 230) recognised classical and sub- classical varieties in the Upper Palaeolithic assemblages. According to him, the classical variety is characterised by the presence of long and slender blades and varied types of burins. The sub-classical variety, on the other hand, presents poorer work-manship. Vidula Jayaswal (PHI 188-93) proceeded from the same premise and classified the industries as crude and fine, taking into consideration the metrical details of the artifacts. Sarma (1981) suggested 3 phase division - Early, Middle and Late. Sarma's suggestion is difficult to sustain in view of the paucity of precise chronological estimates. Murty (1979) divided the industries as Flakeblade, blade and blade-burin variants. Typo-technological evolution with reference to time scale is implicit in these attempts to interpret the variations in the artifactual details.

Following Murty's classification, the Upper Palaeolithic of the Manjra Valley may be described as a 'Flake-Blade' assemblage. It is, rather, a matter of surprise that the middle reaches of the Manjra valley explored by the present writer failed to yield evidences of both the lower and middle Palaeolithic cultures, either on surface or in stratigraphic context. In Manjra Valley the Upper Palaeolithic industry is based on the production of flake tools and blade tools. Chert (71%) was the principal raw-material supplemented by jasper and agate. Flake tools account for 61.29% whereas the blade made ones constitute 35.61% of the assemblage. The tool types include scrapers (48.85%), backed pieces (17.05%), blades (10.59%), borers (4%), burins (4%) and points (4%) and flakes (11.52%). In view of the predominant number of flake tools and scraper types, the Upper Palaeolithic assemblage of the Manjra Valley is categorised as 'Flake-Blade' industry. In the following paragraphs the Manjra industry is studied in comparision with Upper Palaeolithic industries found elsewhere in the country, so as to focus on the nature and work-manship of the artifactual material.

Comparable industries are available at Yerragondapalem (Prakasam District, A.P. 1974), Nallamalai Hills, (Kurnool District, A.P. 1960), Bhokar (Nanded District, Maharashtra), and Wainganga (Chanda District, Maharashtra). The 'Flake-Blade' industries, according to Murty, have thick and broad blades suggesting a primitive stage of blade-tool technology. Scrapers form the predominant element in the assemblage. These, together with other tool types, points and borers are commonly fashioned on flakes or flake like blades. Bhokar in Nanded District (1979) and Wainganga in Chanda District not only yielded the same kind of Upper Palaeolithic assemblage as in the Manjra Valley, but they all belong to the same riverine zone, i.e. Godavari. Joshi and Pappu discovered Upper Palaeolithic factory sites at Bhokar on the top and slopes of a hillock. The artifactual assemblage fashioned on chert, Jasper and chalcedony consists of scrapers, blades, borers, points, knives and burins. There are more number of flakes and flake made tools than blades and blade made tools. The tools are surface occurrences as in the Manjra basin. In Wainganga, on the other hand, Joshi (1966) discovered Upper Palaeolithic artifacts in statigraphic context. The tools are associated with the upper gravel separated from the lower by a deposit of silt. The lower gravel bears Middle Palaeolithic artifacts (Wainganga A). The Upper Palaeolithic assemblage thus stratigraphically succeeds the Middle Palaeolithic and consists of scrapers, points, borers, thick truncated blades and burins, all more or less, similar to the tool types of the Manjra. Joshi considers that Wainganga B would belong to the terminal phase of the Middle Palaeolithic. But Allchins (1968) rightly group the assemblage under the head Upper Palaeolithic. The components of these industrial complexes more or less tally with phase II of Patne (Sali 1974-1980) which is characterised by side and end scrapers, backed pieces and blades. Surface occurrences of Flake-Blade assemblages have been reported from Pratappoor and Marvam (1959-1960) in Palamau District of Bihar. At Dhakulya, Ghosh collected Upper Palaeolithic tools comprising scrapers, blades, points, burins, knives and awls in a Kankar deposit overlying yellowish brown silt. The industry compares well with the Manjra valley Upper Palaeolithic in tool typology.

Yerragondapalem (1974) Prakasam District of A.P., is an important Upper Palaeolithic site. Rallavagu, a small wet weather stream flowing in the vicinity, exposed dark brown silt underlain by pebble gravel. The Upper Palaeolithic tools recovered from the gravel consists of scrapers (58.4%), backed pieces (12.7%), knife edged blades (4.5%), points (11.5%), burins (4.9%), and awls (1.02%). Blades and blade made tools account for 33.86% of the total collection. The artifactual components are more or less similar to that of the Manjra Valley. Another of the comparable area is the Nallamalai Hills where Cammiade and Burkitt (1930) and Isaac (1960) discovered a number of Upper Palaeolithic tool bearing localities. The sites are widely distributed in the area and the general collection consists of scrapers (24.9%), blades (22.4%), borers (12.9%), and burins (6.3%). Fine grained quartzite was the raw material used for tool manufacture. In the Upper reaches of the Paleru Valley (1979), Prakasam District, there is a group of Upper Palaeolithic sites. The assemblages characterised by scrapers (39.21%), blades (36.3%), points (9.1%), borers (3.53%), burins (3.53%) and knives (3.94%). The composition of the assemblage nearly tallies with the Upper Palaeolithic of the Manjra Valley.

From the typological point of view, the above mentioned groups of assemblages are close to that of the Middle Palaeolithic and as such might indicate an early date. The stratified evidence available at Patne too favours an early date for the Flake-Blade type Upper Palaeolithic industries. But chronological consideration needs to take into account regional variation. The available carbon 14 dates from Upper Palaeolithic industries range from 25000 ± 200 at Patne to 10035 ± 125 at Asla. It is difficult to give a more precise date for the Manjra Valley Upper Palaeolithic phase than stating that the industry dates to the time bracket 20000 - 10000 years of age.

MESOLITHIC CULTURE

The Mesolithic culture characterised by microliths is discovered at 33 localities in the Manjra Valley. At three of the sites, Microliths have been found exclusively and at thirty other sites they come in association with the Upper Palaeolithic tools. This cooccurrence of the two industries is taken as evidence for uninterrupted succession of the two industries.

The term Mesolithic has been variously described in Indian context as Epipalaeolithic, Proto-Neolithic and Late Stone Age. Allchins (1968) observe that Microliths occur in sub-soil contexts. These are spread through out the country and occur in varied geomorphic situations. Mishra (1967) classified the Mesolithic sites as littoral, reverine, rock-shelter and open air sites. The available carbon 14 determinations indicate that the Mesolithic phase began some 10000 years ago and continued till the onset of the Neolithic, some 4,500 years ago. Microliths form part of the Neolithic ensemble and in certain areas they were in use even in early historic times (Subba Rao, *Personality of India*). Through this long period of time in which the Microliths were used, the Mesolithic societies under went changes. Some of the changes may be accounted for cultural influences from out side culture areas. It is in this way that the Mesolithic folk acquired pottery and metallurgy. Lal (1958 A14) tried to interpret the Mesolithic evidences in this country under separate heads, Aceramic-Mesolithic and Ceramic-Mesolithic and Non- Geometric and Geometric Microlithic industries. Birbhanpoor (1958), Sanganakallu (Foote 1916; Subba Rao 1948), Teri sites (1956), Sarai Naharrai are among the important examples of aceramic and non-geometric microlithic industries. Langhnaj (Sankalia 1956) and Bagor are among the best known examples for ceramic and geometric microlithic industries. This classification of the Microlithic industry in India has the stratigraphic confirmation from Belan Valley and Lekhania (1930, 1961-63).

The material of Manjra Valley Microlithic is classified as aceramic and non-geometric. The industry is composed of more number of flake made specimens than blade made ones. Of the total number of finished specimens, the flake made ones account for 65.44% while the blade made ones to 32.56% and the core made ones are 2%. Besides this, there are 17 blade blanks and 23 fluted cores. The artifact types include scraper variants (36.14%), backed blades (24.4%), borers (15.12%), blades (8.13%), and scrapers on blades (4.65%) and flakes (4.65%), points (3.45%) and burins (1.43%). The principal raw material was chert (81.37%); other materials being jasper and agate.

A number of Microlithic bearing localities were discovered in different parts of Andhra Pradesh. Foote (1916), Cammiade (1924), Cammiade and Burkitt (1930), Sounder Rajan (1958), Isaac (1960), Nagabhushana Rao (1966), Krishna Murthy (1970) and Kasturibai (1982). Significant among these discoveries were Cammiade's in the lower Godavari Valley. Cammiade pointed out microlithic occurrence at more than 100 sites. At Nagarjunakonda microliths occurred in a two feet thick gravel wash. The assemblage is non- geometric and aceramic. The chief raw materials, as in the Manjra Valley, are chert, jasper and agate. In Kurnool and Prakasam Districts of Andhra Pradesh (Cammiade and Burkitt 1930; and Isaac 1960) microliths occur on surface. Quartz is the chief raw material. The total assemblage consists of scrapers, borers, burins, blades and backed pieces. These are unassociated with the pottery and Geometrics, Trapezes and Triangles. In the lime stone areas of Kurnool district, Murty and Timma Reddi (1976) discovered several microlithic bearing localities, several aceramic and non-geometric microlith bearing localities. The raw materials were jasper, chert, chalcedony, lime stone, quartzite and quartz. Rami Reddi (1975) discovered 14 microlithic sites in the western part of Kurnool and in Anantapur Districts, where the assemblages are without pottery and geometrics. In Nalgonda District S.N. Rao (1966) discovered several microlithic factory sites. Pottery and geometrics were absent at the localities.

In Shorapur, Karnataka, Paddaiah (1968-1970, 1971, 1972, 1974) discovered over 30 microlithic sites. The sites are rich in artifactual yield and there occur geometric as well, though not in good numbers. The industry is thus not comparable with that of the Manjra Valley. At Sanganakallu, Subba Rao (1948) discovered microlithic industry of Pre-neolithic age. After a detailed survey in the area, Majumdar and Rajaguru (1966) pointed out that the microlithic horizon sandwiched between the Upper Palaeolithic and Neolithic. Sankalia (1974) dated the industry from 9000-3000 B.C.. The artifacts were made on both blade and flakes and comprised of scrapers, retouched and blunted blades, points, awls, burins and lunates. There were neither geometrics nor pottery. The Sanganakallu industry thus tallies with that of the Manjra Valley.

The Teri sites (Zeuner and Allchin 1956) are among the best known microlithic bearing localities in Tamilnadu. Quartz and chert were employed in nearly equal proportion for tool manufacture. The Teri's industry comprises backed and obliquely blunted blades, scraper variants, variety of points, lunates, traingles, chopping tools and discoids and blade cores. A distinctive feature of the industry is the presence of pressure flaked, bifacial points. The Mesolithic phase of the Teri sites is dated to about 4000 B.C. The Manjra industry, like that of the Teri's, though aceramic, does not possess geometrics.

Around Bombay, Todd (1950) discovered several Mesolithic sites. The artifacts occur on rock outcrops. These industries composed of blades, backed pieces, triangles, trapezes, drills, scrapers, mace-heads etc., are clearly rich, variegated and more advanced than that of the Manjra industry. At Patne (Sali 1980) the microlithic culture occupies 3m. thick deposit. A three phased evolution of the Mesolithic culture is outlined on the basis of available stratigraphical evidence. But the Patne industry comprising both geometric and crested ridge blades is more sophisticated than that of the Manjra Valley.

The above factual evidences clearly indicate that the Manjra Valley microlithic industry is of a primitive and unsophisticated variety. Though no precise dates are available, the Manjra Valley Mesolithic culture may be dated to the time bracket of 9000-4000 B.C. on the basis of the observations made with respect to a similar industrial complex at Sanganakallu.

REFERENCES

Allchin, Bridget & Remond	1968	*The Birth of Indian Civilization.*
— & Hegde, K.T.M.	1968	The Back ground of Early Man in the Narmada Valley, Gujarat. *The Journal of the M.S.University of Baroda* - Vol. XII No. 1.
— & Goudie, A	1971	Dunes, Aridity and early Man in Gujarat Western India, *Man* 6
—	1974	World Archaeology Vol. 5.
Subba Rao, B.	1948	*Stone Age Culture of Bellary,* Poona.
—	1949	*Prehistory and Early Historic Bellary.* Ph.D. Unpublished Thesis, Deccan College Libraries.
—	1958	*The Personality of India,* 2nd Edition, Baroda.
Cammiade, L.A. & Burkitt, M.C.	1930	Fresh Light on the Stone Ages in South East India. *Antiquity* Vol. IV.
De Terra, H & Paterson, T.T.	1939	*Studies on the Ice Age in India and Associated Human Cultures,* Washington.

Flint, R.F.	1963	Pleistocene Climates in low altitude, *Geographical Review,* 53-1.
Foote, R.B.		*Prehistoric and Protohistoric Antiquities of India.*
Ghosh, A.	1948	Prehistoric Explorations in India, *IHC* 24
Ghosh, A.K.	1961	Prehistoric studies in Eastern India, SC. *Cul* 27.
Sen, D & Ghosh, A.D.— (Eds.)	1966	Implements from Late Site in Eastern India in *Studies in Prehistory* B.R. Foote Memorial Volume, Calcutta.
—	1970	*The Palaeolithic Culture of Singhbhum* Transection of the American Philosophical Society.
Hegde, K. Tm.M.	1972	Physics and Chemistry in Indian Archaeology *Archaeological Congress* and Seminar Papers (Ed. S.B. Deo) Nagpur, pp. 133-141.
Joshi, R.V. & Khare, M.D.	1966	Microlithic bearing Deposits of Adamgarh Rock Shelters in *Studies in Prehistory* Eds. D.Sen and A.K. Ghosh, Calcutta, 90-95.
Joshi & Bopardikar, B.P.	1972	Stone Age cultures of Konkan in *Archaeological Congress* and Seminar Papers Ed. S.B. Deo, Nagpur 47-51.
	1973	*The Significance of Microlithic tools in Post Palaeolithic Industries.*
Khan, E	1968	Pleistocene stratigraphy in India. *Annals of the Geology Department* Vol-IV, Alligarh.
Joshi, R.V.	1978	*Stone Age cultures of Central India,*

		Deccan College, Post Graduate and Research Institute, Poona.
Joshi, R.V.	1979	Bhokar - A upper Palaeolithic Factory Site from Central Godavary Basin, Maharashtra, *Man and Environment, III.*
Chittale, Rajaguru, S.V. Pappu, S.N. & Badam, R.S.	1981	Archaeological Studies in the Manjra Valley, Central Godavary basin, *Bulletin of Deccan College,* Research Institute.
Srinivasan, L.K.	1960-61	*Indian Archaeology*-A. Review.
Lal, B.B.	1958	Birbhampoor, A microlithic site in the Damodar Valley, West Bengal, *AI* - Vol. 4.
Murthy, M.L.K.	1966	*The Stone Age cultures of Chittoor District,* Ph.D. Unpublished Thesis; Poona University.
—	1968	Blade and Burin Industries near Renigunta on South East Coast of India, *Proceedings of Prehistoric Society* (N.S.) XXXIV 83-101.
—	1970	Blade and Burin and Late Stone Age Industries, around Renigunta, Chittoor District *I.A*.4.
—	1974	A Late Pleistocene Cave Site in Southern Indian PA. Ps.
—	1974	Late Pleistocene Fauna of Kurnool Caves, South India, in A.T. Clason (Ed) *Archaeological Studies* (Amastardam)
Thimma Reddi, K.	1976	The significance of Lithic Finds in Cave areas of Kurnool ***Asian Perspectives*** 18.
Murthy, M.L.K.	1979	Recent research in the Upper Palaeolithic Phase in India, *Journal of field Archaeology*.

Seshadri, M.	1953	Microlithic Idustries of Mysore, Arluta, 9.
—	1954	Microlithic Industries of Kibbanahalli, Mysore State *C.S.* XXIII
—	1956	*The stone using cultures of Prehistoric and Protohistoric Mysore,* London.
Malik, S.C.	1956 to 1957	*Indian Archaeology-A Review*
Misra, V.N.	1977	*Prehistoric Man and His Art in Central India.*
Madhusudhana Rao	1979	*Stone Age cultures of Paleru River valley, Prakasam District, Andhra Pradesh,* Unpublished Thesis, Nagarjuna University.
Kasturibai, M.	1982	*The Stone Age culstrures of the Eleru Valley in East Godavary District, Andhra Pradesh,* Ph.D. unpublished Thesis, Nagarjuna University.
Paddaiah, K.	1968	*Pre and Protohistoric Investigations in Shorapur Doab,* Ph.D. Unpublished Thesis, Poona University.
—	1970	The Blade Tool Industry of Shorapur Doab, Penninsular India, *I.A.* 4.
—	1974	Pre and Protohistoric finds from Salvadgi hills, Bijapoor district, Karnataka, *Journal of the University of Poona* (Humanities Section) 41.
Pappu, R.S.	1966	*Pleistocene Studies in the upper Krishna Basin,* Ph.D. Thesis, Deccan College.
Raman, K.V.	1960 to 1961	*IAR* 1960-61
Rajaguru, S.N. and Hegde, K.T.M.	1972	The Pleistocene stratigraphy in India, *Archaeological Concgress and Seminar Papers* (Ed.S.B. Deo) Nagpur, 74.
Rajaguru, S.N.	1973	Pleistocene climatic changes in Western

India, *Radio Carbon and Indian Archaeology* (Eds. D.B. Agarwal, A. Ghosh)

Rikes, R. 1967 *Water, Weather and Prehistory;* London.

Ramireddy, V. 1968 *Pre and Protohistory of South Western Andhra Pradesh,* Ph.D., Unpublished Thesis, Poona.

— 1975 The Meosolithic cultures in Kurnool and Anantapur Districts, South India, *The Journal of the Karnataka University.*

Ramireddy, V. 1976 *The prehistoric and protohistoric cultures of Palvoy, South India.*

Sankalia, H.D. 1956 The Microlithic Industry of Langhnaj, in Gujarat Middle stone age culture.

1963 In India and Pakistan, *Science No.* 146.

1965 Excavations at Langhnaj 1944-63.

— 1969 Mesolithic and Pre-Mesolithic Industry from the excavation at Sanganakallu, Bellary, 1965, Deccan College, Poona,

— 1974 *Prehistory and Protohistory of India and Pakistan.*

Sharma, M.J. 1982 *The Upper Palaeolithic culture of India,* Agamkala Prakasan. Delhi.

Soundara Rajan, K.V. 1950 Stone Age Industries Near Giddalur, District Kurnool, *A.I.*No.8.

— 1958 Studies in Stone Ages of Nagarjuna Konda and Its Neighbourhood *AI.* 14.

Rao S.N. 1966 *Stone Age Cultures of Nalgonda* Ph.D. Unpublished Thesis Poona University, Deccan College Libraries.

Sali, S.A. 1970 IA 4

	1974	Upper Palaeolithic researches since Independence *Bulletin of the Deccan College,* 34.
	1980	*Stone Age Culture sequence at Patne, District Jalgaon, Maharasthra,* Ph.D. Thesis, University of Poona.
Sharma , G. R.	1956-57	IAR pp 11-15
	1964-65	—
	1973	Mesolithic cultures in the Ganga Valley, India. Proceeding of the Prehistoric Society, 39.
	1975	Seasonal Migrations and Mesolithic Lake culture of the Ganga Valley, *Presidential Address, Indian Prehistoric Society,* Delhi.
—	1980	Archaeology of the Ganga Valley, History to Prehistory.
Vita Fing	1971	Heridity and Environment in Plastic sediments: Silt/clay depletion, Geological Society of America, Bulletin, 82.
Vidula Jayaswal	—	Palaeohistory of India
—	1973	*Study of the Prepared core Technics in Palaeolothic cultures of India,* Unpublished Thesis, Banaras Hindu University.
Wain Wright, C.A.	1964	*The Pleistocene deposit of the Lower Narmada river and an early stone age India from the river Chambal,* Baroda.
Zeuner, F.E. & Allchin, B.		Microlithic sites in Tinnevelly District, Madras State. AI, 12.

SELECT BIBLIOGRAPHY

ANDERSON, C.W. 1917 Notes on Prehistoric Implements found in the Singhbhum District; JBORS, 3 : 349-362.

ANSARI, Z.D. & NAGARJA RAO, M.S. 1969 Excavations at Sanganakallu, (1964-65) Deccan College, Poona.

BORDES, FRACOISE 1968 The old Stone Age, World University Library, London.

BROWN, COGGIN 1917 Catalogue of Prehistoric Antiquities in the Indian Museum at Calcutta, Simla.

BURKITT, M.C. 1963 The Old Stone Age - A study of Palaeolithic Times.

CAMMIADE, L.A. 1924 Pygmy Implements of the Lower Godavari, *Man in India* 4 : 83-105

CAMMIADE, L.A. & BURKITT M.C. 1930 Fresh Light on the Stone Age of South East India, Antiquity, 4 : 327-339.

DANI, A.H. 1960 *Prehistory and Protohistory of Eastern India,* Calcutta.

FOOTE, R.B. 1866 On the occurrence of Stone Implements in various parts of Madras and North Arcot Districts, MOLS, III Series.

1914 The Foote's Collection of Indan Prehistoric Antiquities, Madras.

1916 The Foote Collection of Indian Prehistoric and Protohistoric Antiquities -Notes on thier Ages and Distribution, Madras.

GHOSH, A. 1948 Prehistoric Explorations in India, IHC 24 (1) 1-18.

GORDON, D.H. 1950 The Stone Industries of the Holocene in India and Pakistan, Ancient India 6 : 64-90.

ISAAC, N. 1960 The Stone Age cultures of Kurnool, Ph.D. Unpublished Thesis, Poona University and Deccan College Libraries.

JOSHI, R.V. 1978 Stone Age Cultures of Central India, Deccan College, Postgraduate and Research Institute, Poona.

KHATRI, A.P. 1961 Stone Age and Pleistocene Chronology of the Narmada valley, (Central India), *Anthronos*, 56 : 519-530.

KRISHNASWAMI, V.D.1947 Stone Age in India, AI. 3 : 11-57.

1952 Progress in prehistory AI. 9: 53-79.

KRISHNASWAMI, V.D. & SOUNDARA RAJAN, K.V. 1951 The Lithic Tool-Industries of the Singrauli Basin, District Mirzapur, AI. 7: 40-65.

LYDEKKER, R; 1886 a Preliminary Note on the Mammalia of Kurnool Caves RGSI 19: 2.

1886 b The Fauna of Kurnool caves, *Palasontolonis* India, Series × 4 :2 : 22-58.

MALTI NAGAR	1975	Role of Ethnographic evidence in the reconstruction of Archaeological data, The *Eastern Anthropologist,* 28 (1) : 13-22.
MISRA, V.N.	1962	Problems of Terminology in Indian Prehistory, *Eastern Anthropologist,* 15 (2) : 113-124.
	1967	Pre-and Proto-history of the Berach Basin South Rajasthan, Deccan College, Poona.
MISRA, V.N. & M. NAGAR	1973	Twenty-five years of Indian Prehistory (1947-1972) a Review of Reaserch, in *Man and Society, Lucknow,* Ed.by K.S. Mathur: 1-54.
MISRA, V.N.	1973	Bagor-a late Mesolithic Settlement in North-West India, *World Archaeology,* 5(1) : 92 : 110.
MOONE, H.V.V.	1934	A classification of Flint Burins or Gravers, PPSLXIV : 81-92.
MUTTON, JH.	1928	Prehistory of Assam, *Man in India,* 88 : 228-229.
NAIDU, A.S.	1966	Lithological and Chemical Facies changes in the Recent Deltaic sediments of the Godavari River, India; 'Deltas'in their geologic frame-work published by Houston Geological Society, U.S.A.
PADDAIAH, K.	1974	Pre-and-Protohistoric finds from Salvadgi hills, Bijapur District, Karnataka, *Journal of the University of Poona,* (Humanities Section) 41 : 109-43.
RAJAGURU, S.N.	1973	On the problem of Late Pleis-

tocens climate changes in Western Maharashtra, in *Radiocarbon and Indian Archaeology* Ed. D.P. Agrawal and A. Ghosh, Bombay, 80-84.

1981 Problem of Late L Pleistocene Aridity in India, VIII Indian Society for Prehistoric and Quaternary Studies.

RAMI REDDY, V. 1968 *Pre and Proto-History of South Western Andhra Pradesh,* Ph.D., unpublished thesis, Poona Libraries.

SANKALIA, H.D. 1956 *The Microlithic Industry of Langhnai,* Gujarat.

1964 *Stone Age Tools, their techniques, Names and probable functions,* Deccan College, Poona.

1965 Excavations at Langhnai, 1944-63 part I, Archaeology, Poona.

SESHADRI, M. 1953 Microlithic Industries of Mysore, ARLUTA 9 : 29-38

1954 Microlithic Industry of Kibbanahalli, Mysore State CS XXIII : 326-7.

1956 *The Stone Using cultures of Prehistoric and Protohistoric Mysore,* London.

SHARMA, G.R. 1973 Mesolithic Cultures in the Ganga valley, India, Proceedings of the Prehistoric Society, 39 : 129-46.

SHARAM, T.C. 1974 Recent Archaeological discoveries in North Eastern India, *Puratattva,* 7 : 17-19.

SMITH, V. 1906 Pigmy implements, *Indian Antiquary,* 35 : 185-96.

SUBBA RAO, B. 1948 *Stone Age cultures of Bellary,* Poona.

SUBRAHMANYAM, B.R. *Excavation of Jami. Visakhapatnam District* (in press)

'Prehistory ' chapter II in *Comprehensive History of Andhra Pradesh* (In press)

VARMA, R.K. 1974 a The Upper Palaeolithic Industry of the Belan Valley paper read in the Symposium of Indian Prehistory 1974, Organised by the Deccan College, Pune (unpublished).

MAPS AND FIGURES

FIG-1

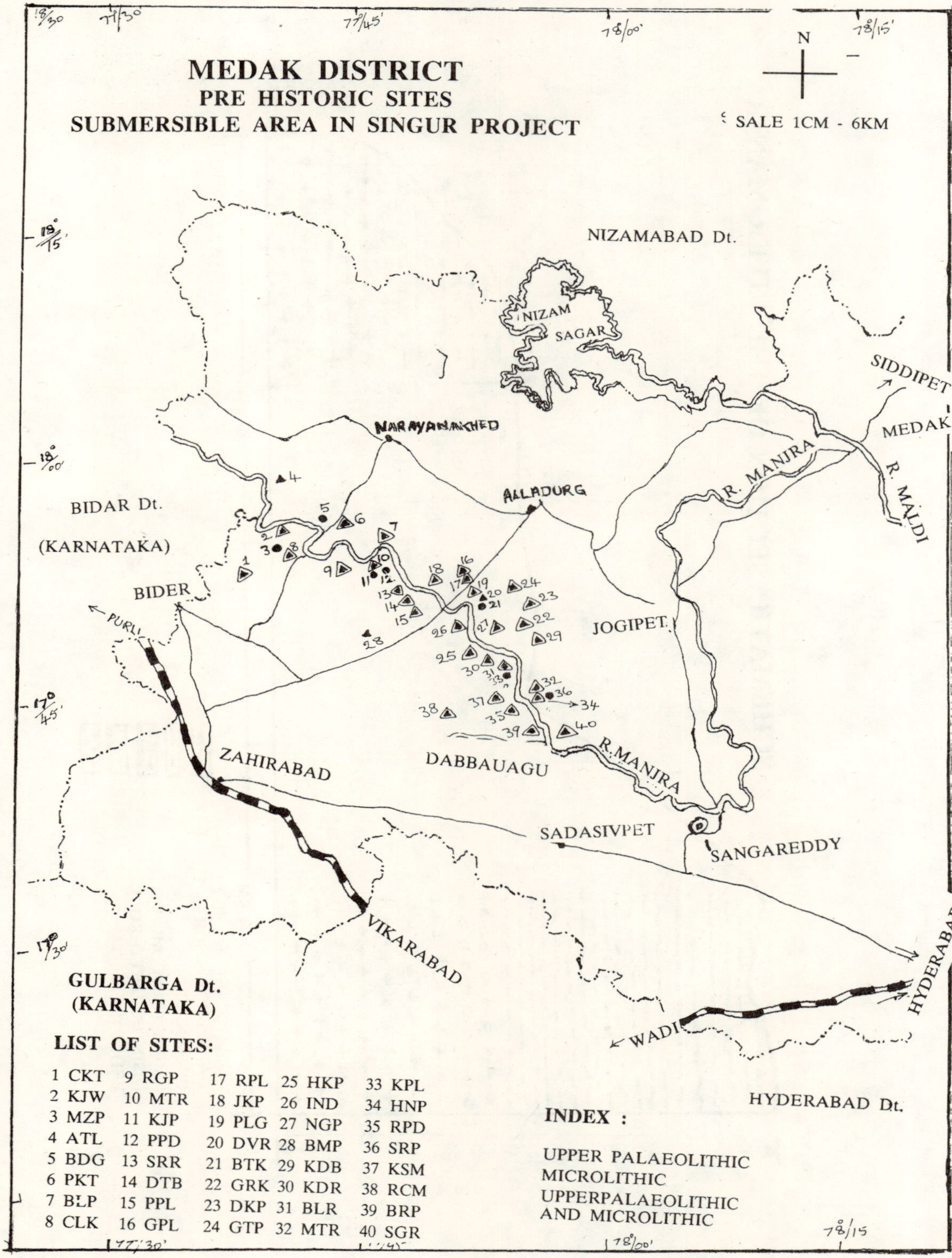

MEDAK DISTRICT
PRE HISTORIC SITES
SUBMERSIBLE AREA IN SINGUR PROJECT
N
SALE 1CM - 6KM
NIZAMABAD Dt.
NIZAM SAGAR
SIDDIPET
MEDAK
R. MALDI
R. MANJRA
NARAYANAKHED
ALLADURG
BIDAR Dt.
(KARNATAKA)
BIDER
PURLI
JOGIPET
DABBAUAGU
R. MANJRA
ZAHIRABAD
SADASIVPET
SANGAREDDY
VIKARABAD
HYDERABAD
WADI
HYDERABAD Dt.
GULBARGA Dt.
(KARNATAKA)
LIST OF SITES:
1 CKT 9 RGP 17 RPL 25 HKP 33 KPL
2 KJW 10 MTR 18 JKP 26 IND 34 HNP
3 MZP 11 KJP 19 PLG 27 NGP 35 RPD
4 ATL 12 PPD 20 DVR 28 BMP 36 SRP
5 BDG 13 SRR 21 BTK 29 KDB 37 KSM
6 PKT 14 DTB 22 GRK 30 KDR 38 RCM
7 BLP 15 PPL 23 DKP 31 BLR 39 BRP
8 CLK 16 GPL 24 GTP 32 MTR 40 SGR
INDEX :
UPPER PALAEOLITHIC
MICROLITHIC
UPPERPALAEOLITHIC AND MICROLITHIC

FIG-2

SCHEMATIC SECTION OF THE RIVER MANJRA

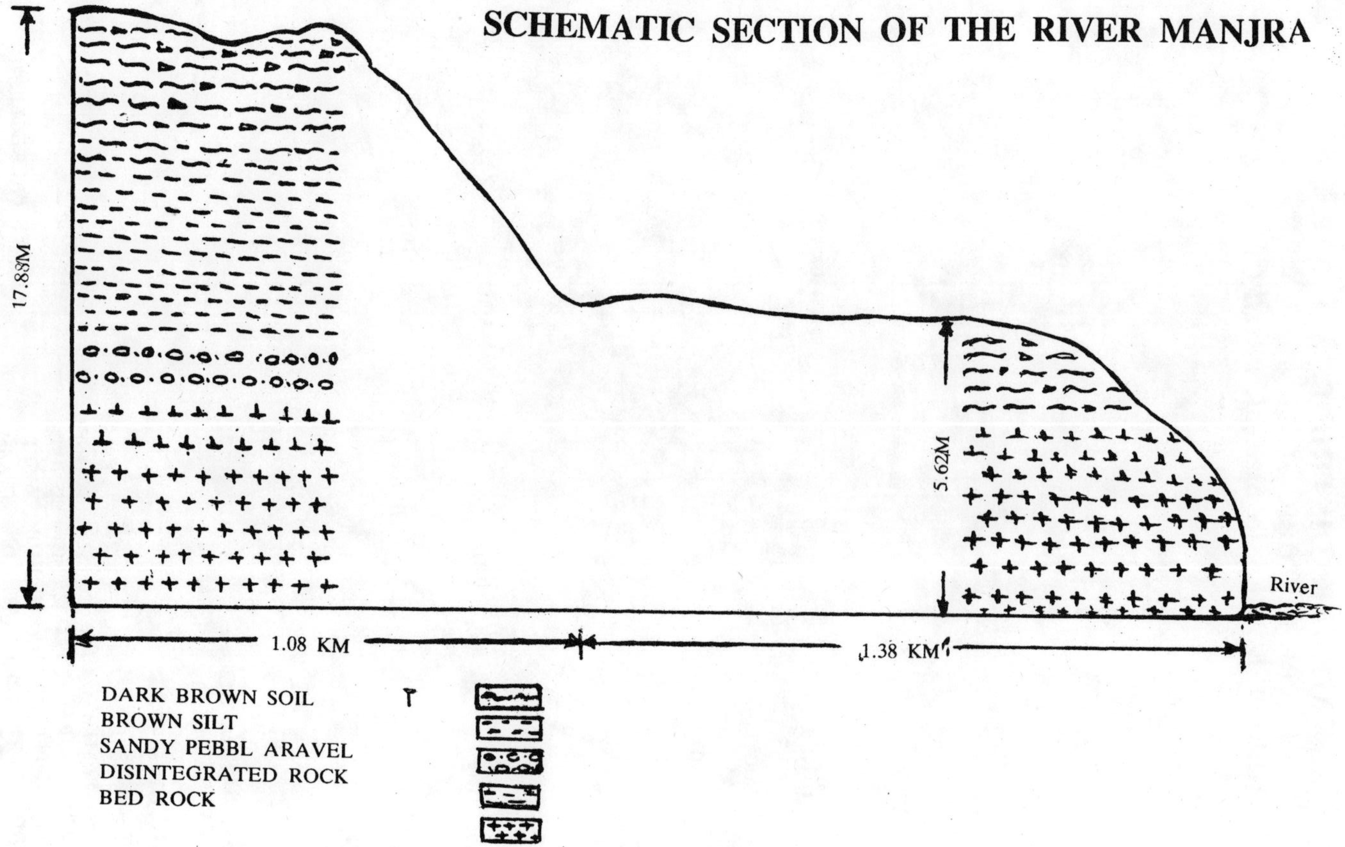

FIG-3

SECTION AT RAIPALLI SITE

DARK BROWN SOIL
WITH CALICH ES.
DISINTIGRATED ROCK

RAIN GOLLI SECTION MURTUZAPUR

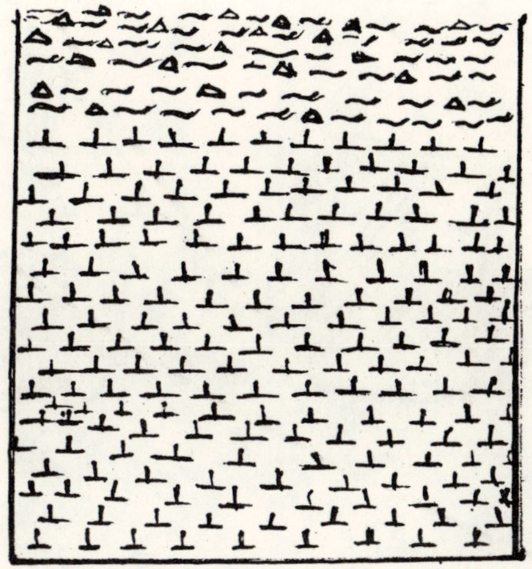

DARK BROWN SOIL
DISINTIGRATED ROCK

FIG-4

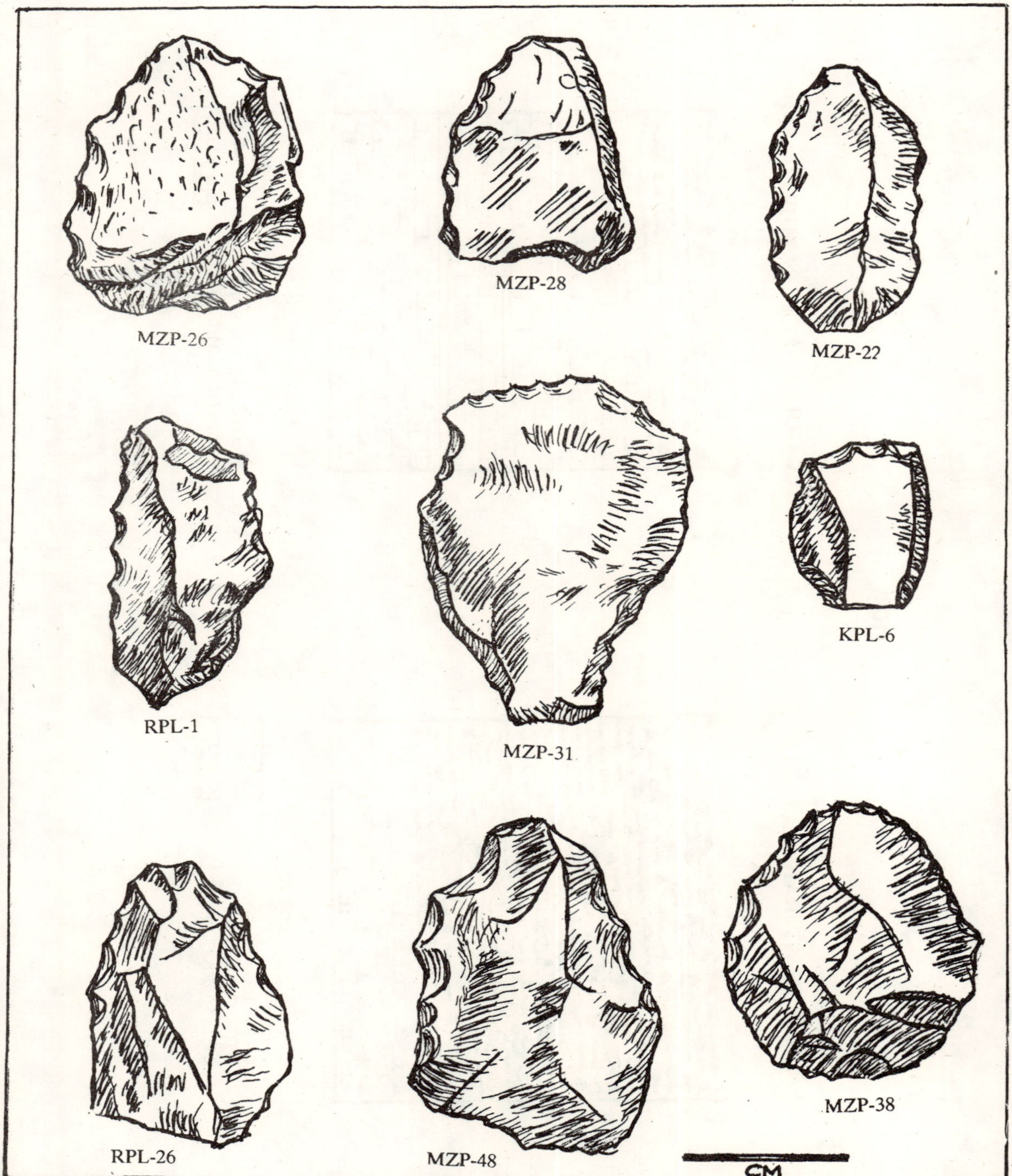

FIG-5

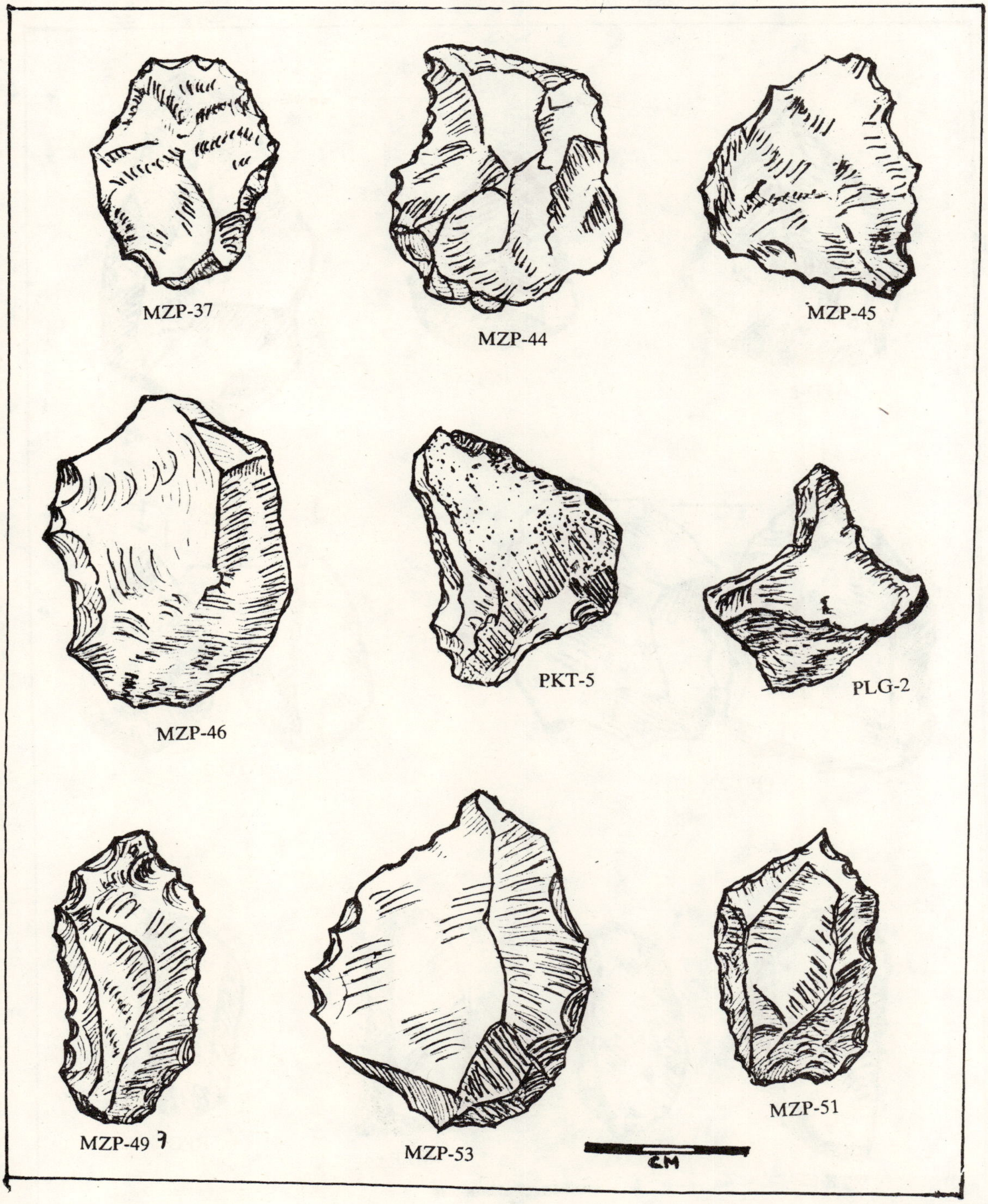

FIG-6

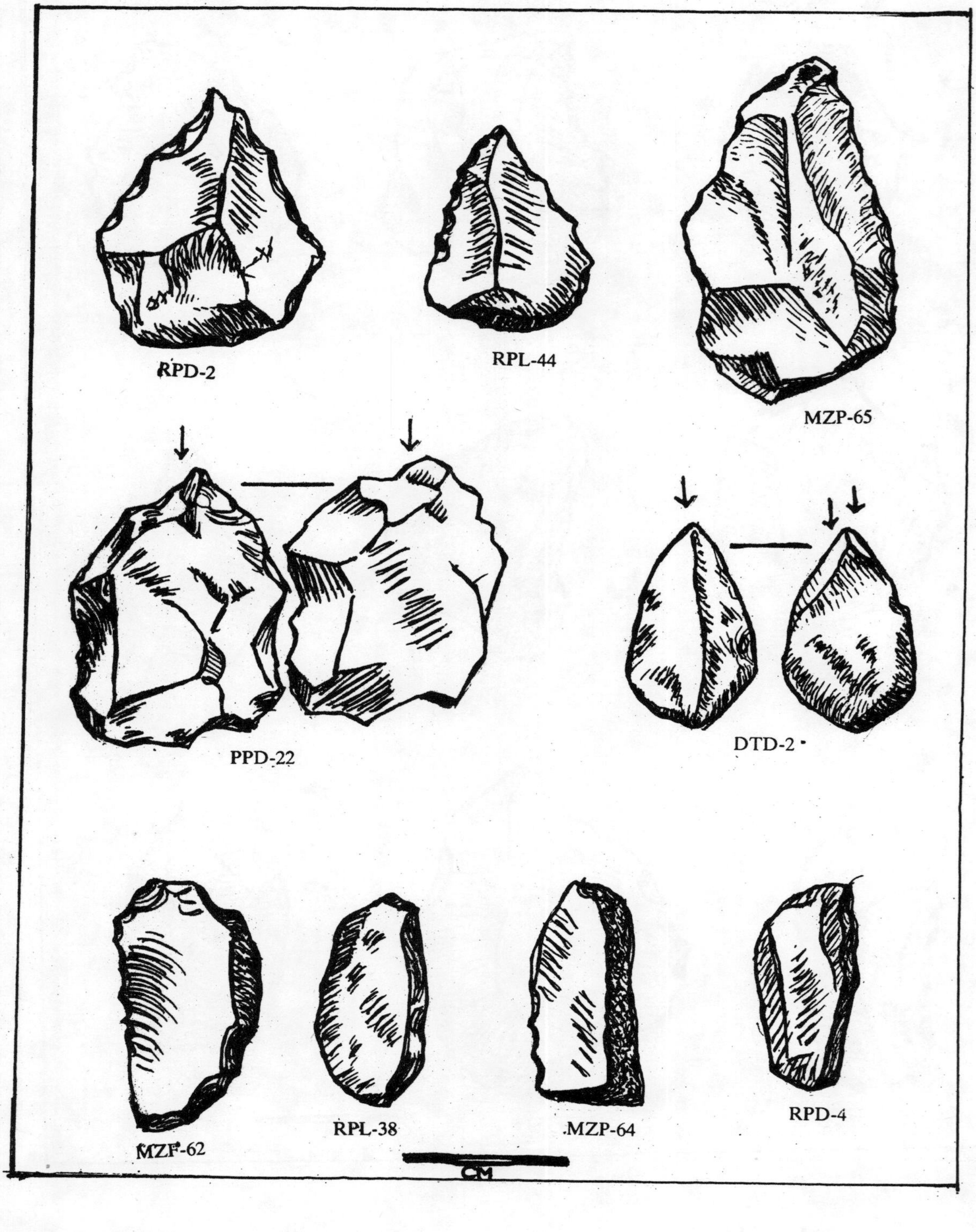

FIG-7

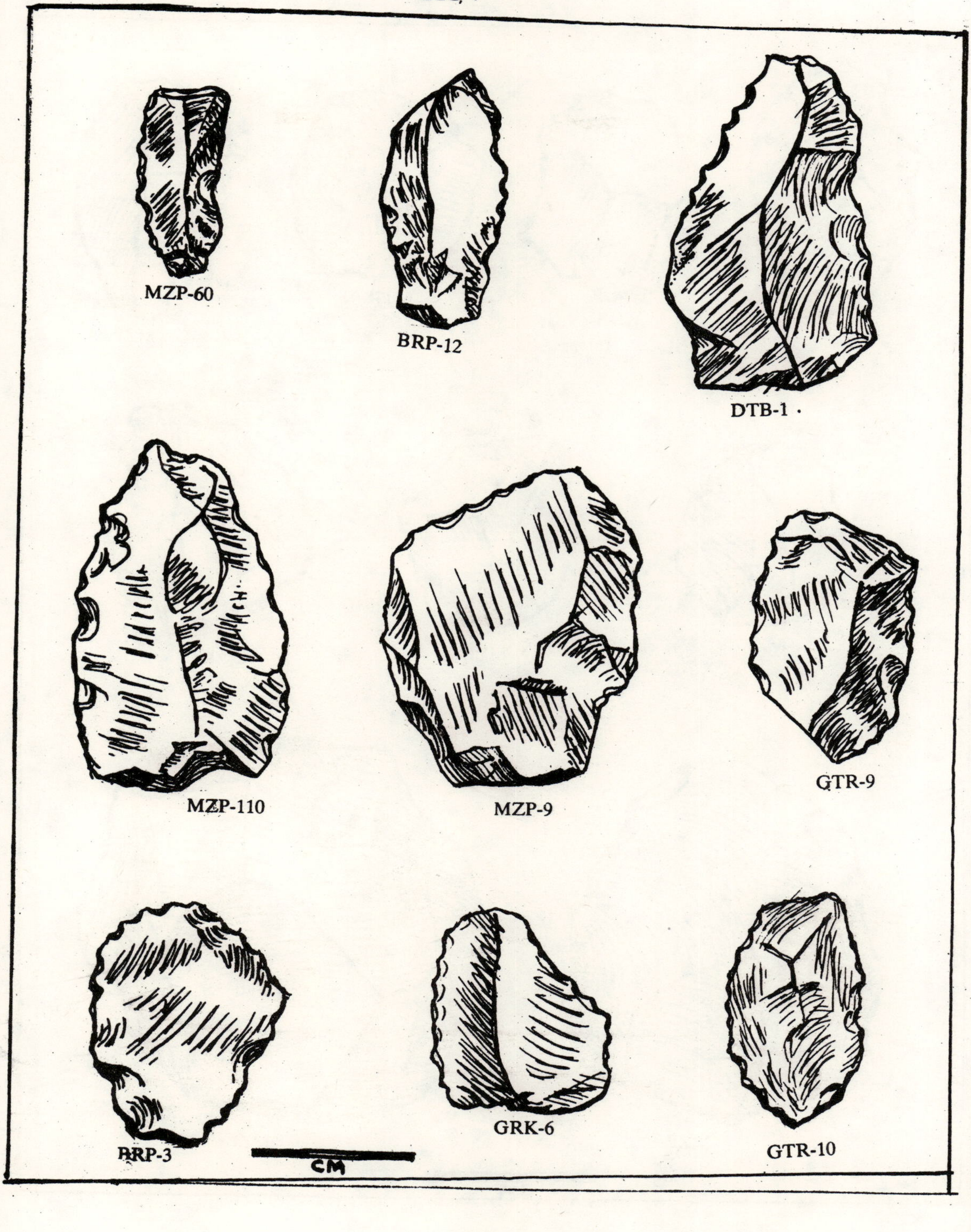

FIG-8

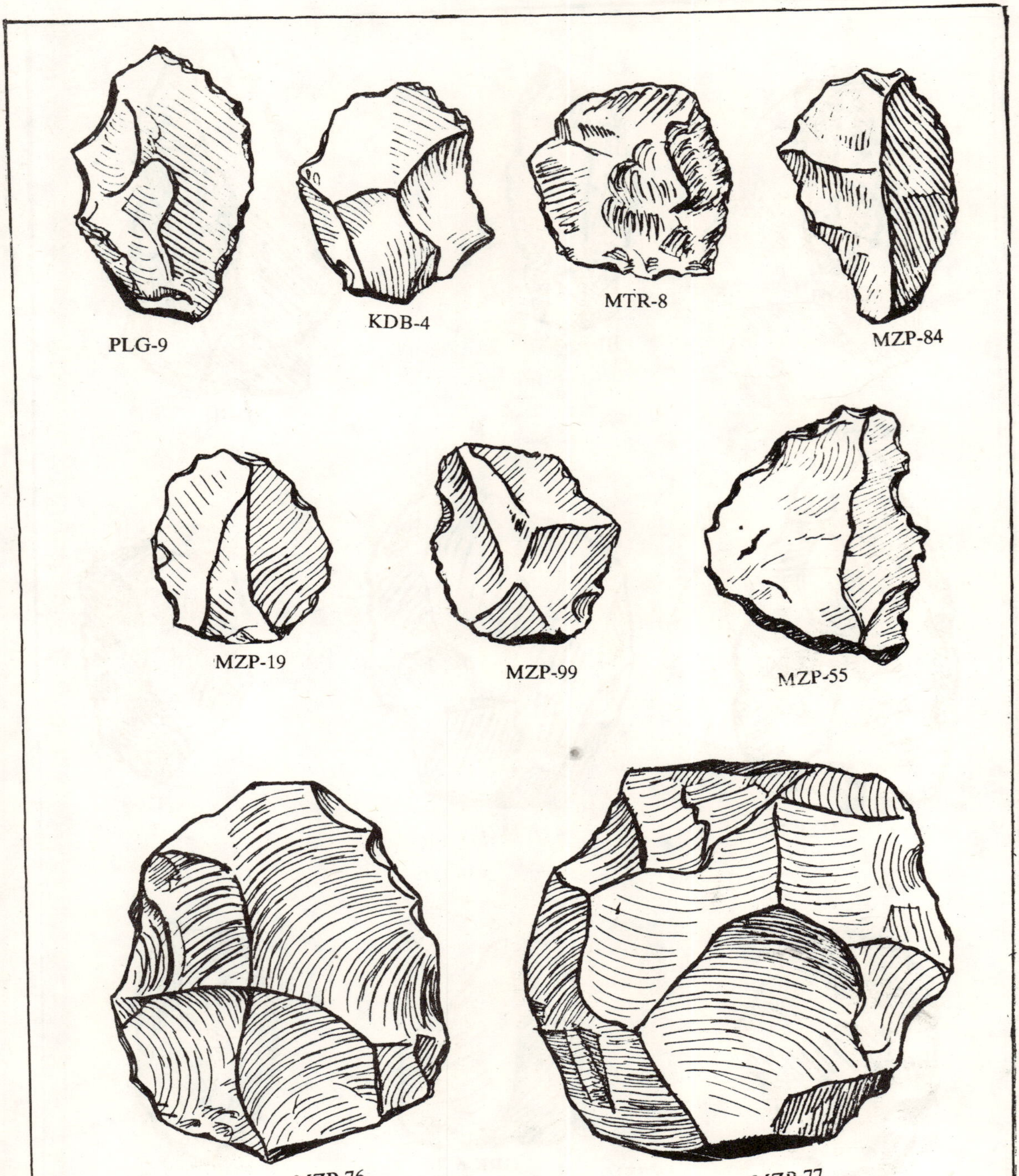

FIG-9

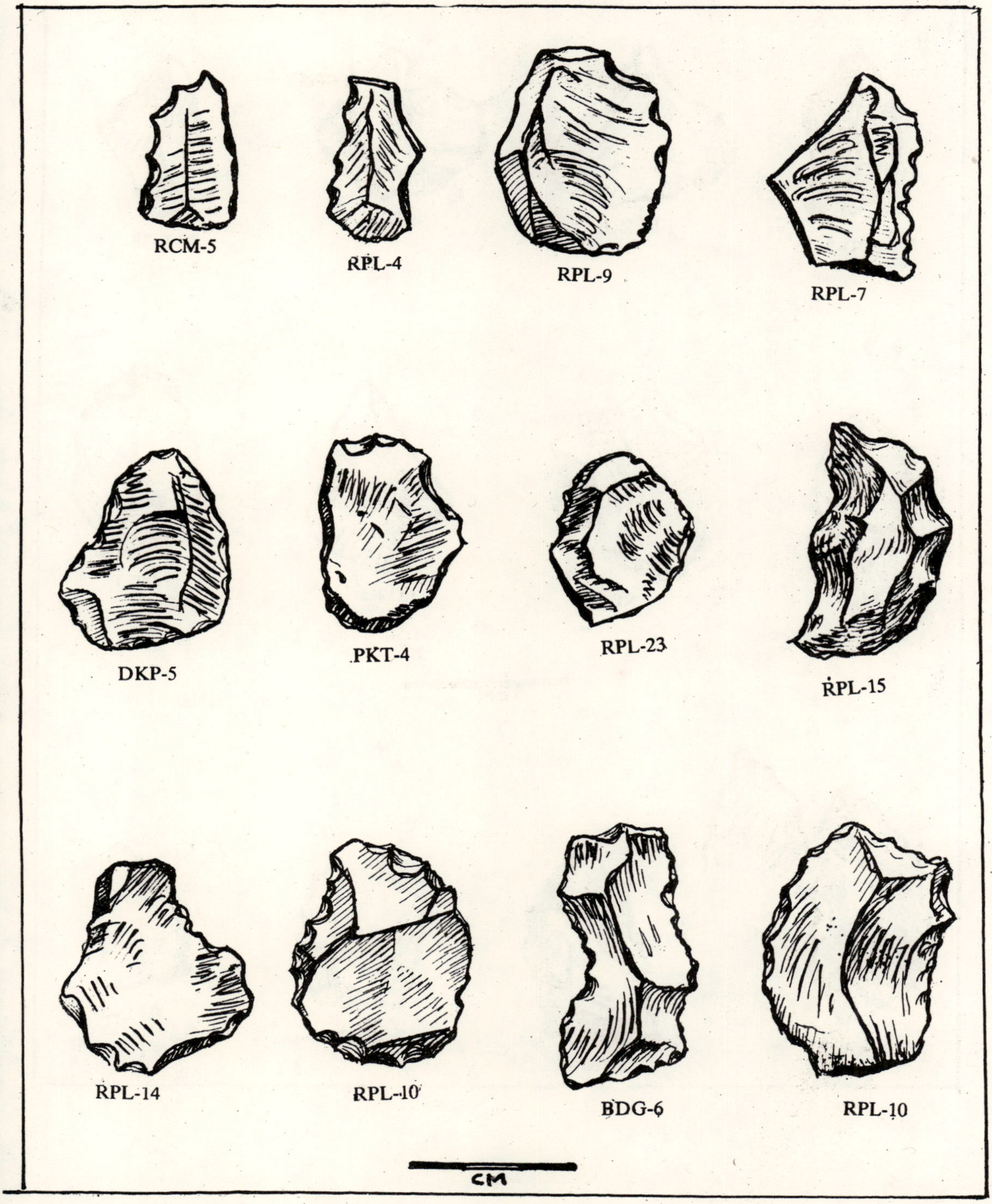
RCM-5
RPL-4
RPL-9
RPL-7
DKP-5
PKT-4
RPL-23
RPL-15
RPL-14
RPL-10
BDG-6
RPL-10
CM

FIG-10

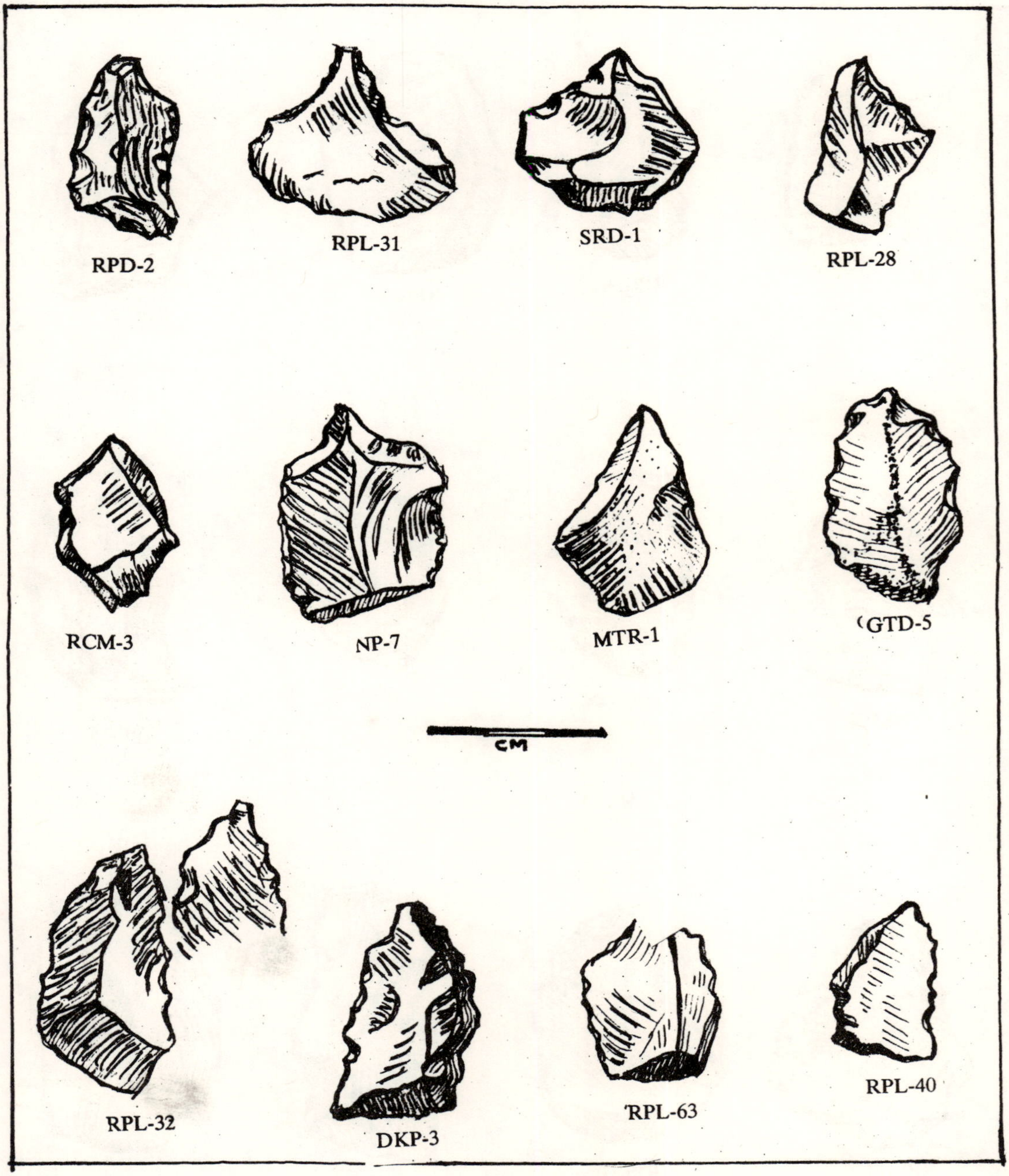
RPD-2
RPL-31
SRD-1
RPL-28
RCM-3
NP-7
MTR-1
GTD-5
CM
RPL-32
DKP-3
RPL-63
RPL-40

FIG-11

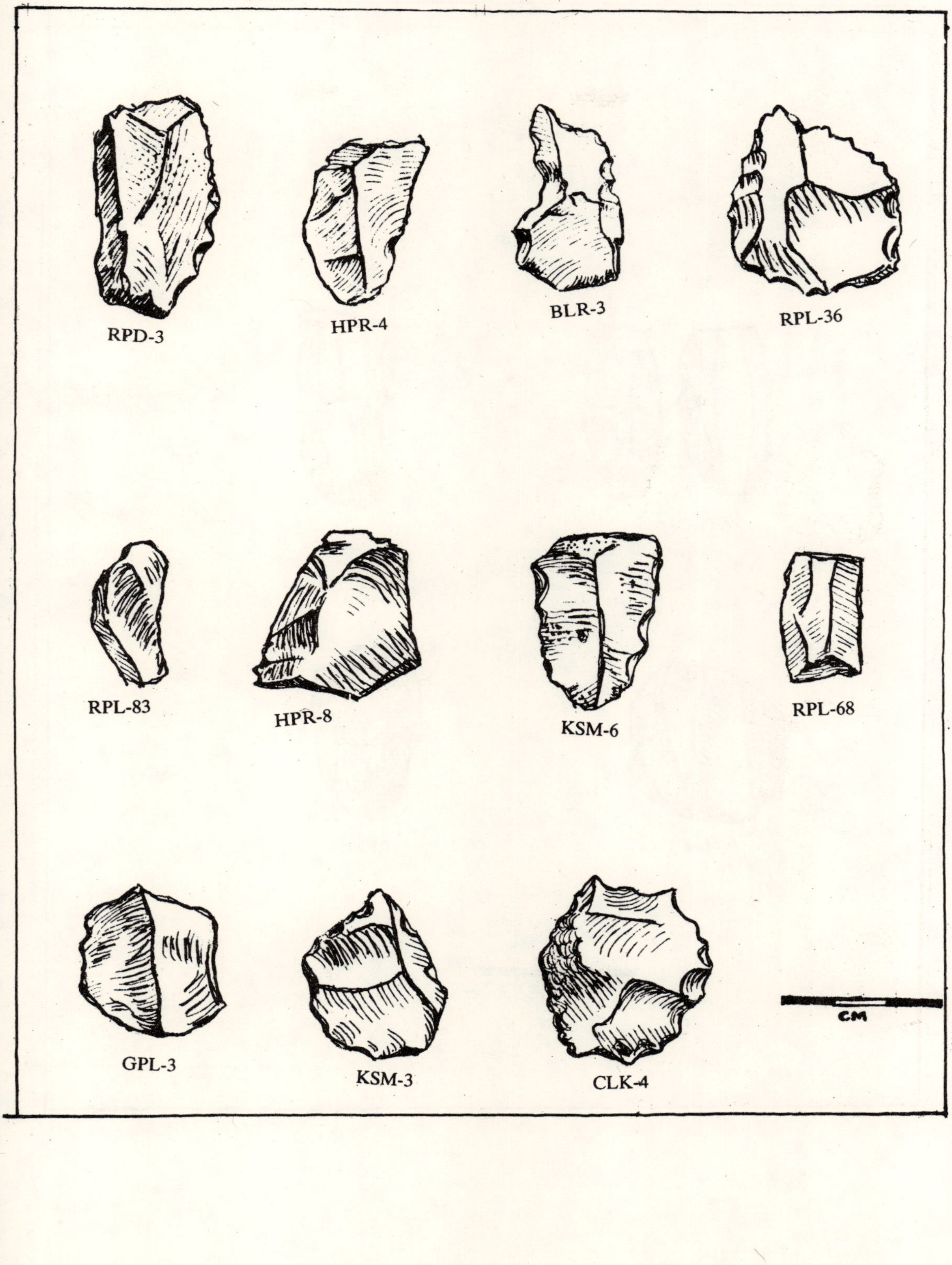

FIG-12

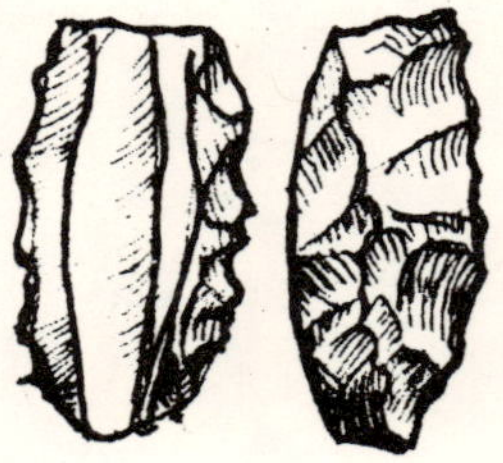

ATL-2

KDB-1

ATL-1

RPL-61

FIG. 13.

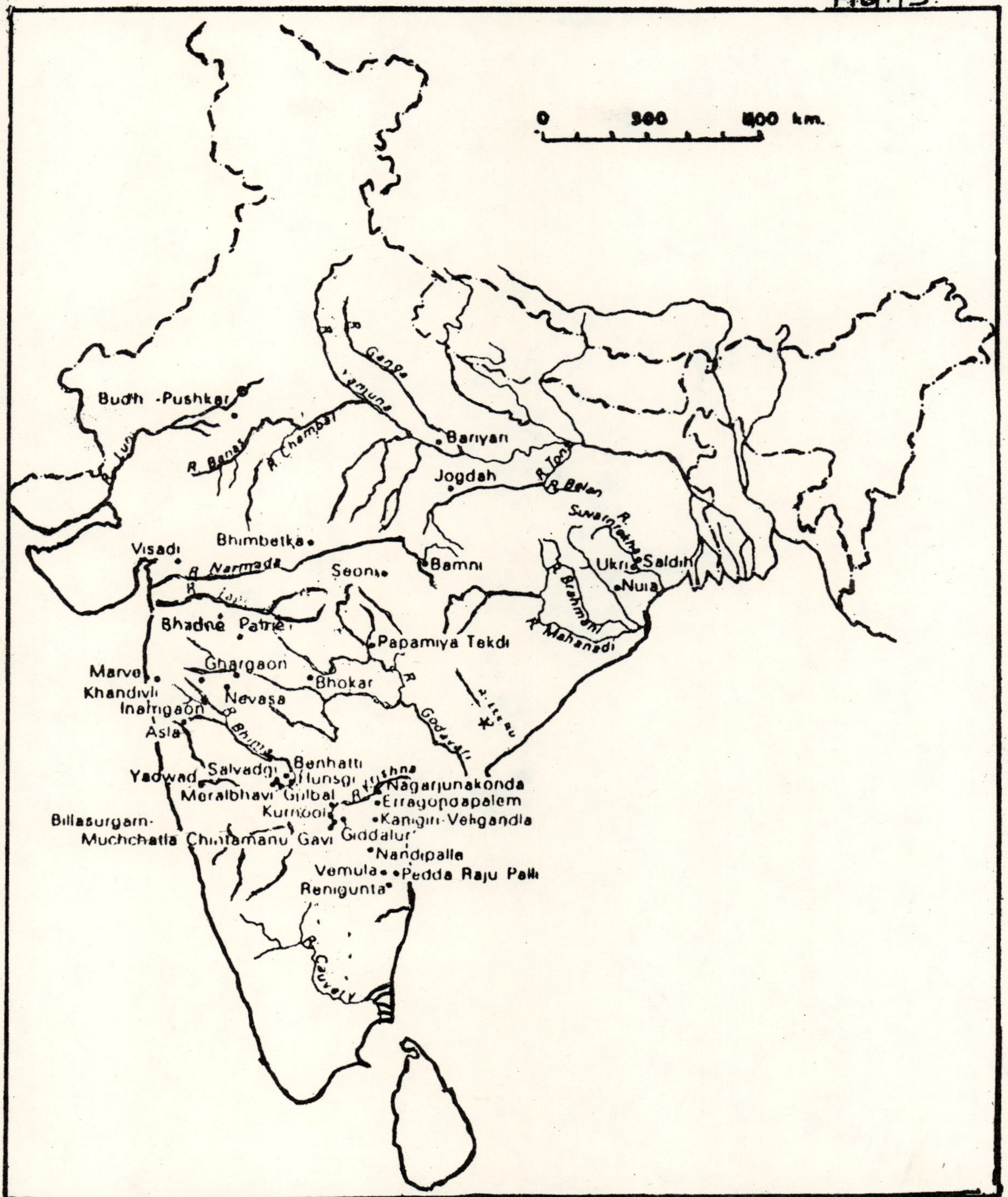

Map showing important Upper Palaeolithic sites in India

Plates

Plates

The Manjra river at Singoor 1

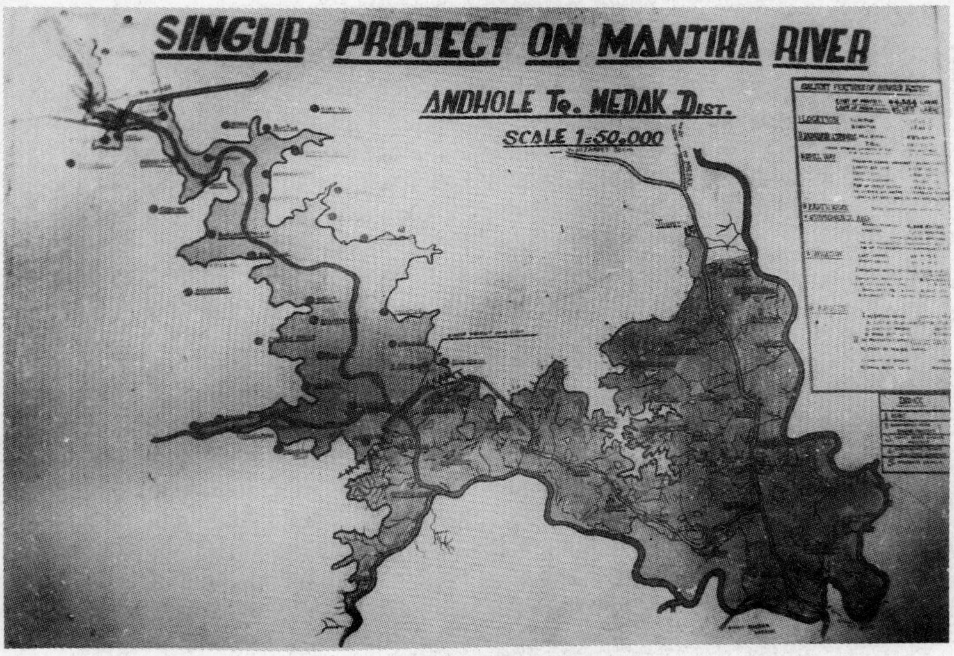

Submersible area under Singoor project 1

Rock exposures on the river bank at Raipalli 2

Rain gully section at Murtuzapoor 2

Chert out crop at Murtuzapoor 3

Working Floor with boulder and artifacts around 3

The surface of the site at Raipalli 4

Upper palaeolithic tools 4

Upper palaeolithic tools 5

Microlithic tools 5